Workbook

Contemporary Economics

William A. McEachern

THOMSON

SOUTH-WESTERN

Australia · Canada · Mexico · Singapore · Spain · United Kingdom · United States

THOMSON

SOUTH-WESTERN

Contemporary Economics Workbook

William A. McEachern

VP/Editorial Director:
Jack W. Calhoun

VP/Editor-in-Chief:
Dave Shaut

Senior Publisher:
Karen Schmohe

Executive Editor:
Eve Lewis

Project Manager:
Carol Sturzenberger

Consulting Editor:
Jeanne Busemeyer/Hyde Park
Publishing Services

VP/Director of Marketing:
Carol Volz

Marketing Manager:
Nancy A. Long

Marketing Coordinator:
Angela Russo

Production Editor:
Darrell E. Frye

Production Manager:
Patricia Matthews Boies

Manufacturing Coordinator:
Kevin Kluck

Design Project Manager:
Stacy Jenkins Shirley

Cover Designer:
Grannan Graphic Design, Ltd.

Cover Images:
© David Muir/Masterfile and Ian
McKinnell/Getty Images

Printer:
Von Hoffmann Graphics
Frederick, MD

For permission to use material from this
text or product, submit a request online
at http://www.thomsonrights.com. Any
additional questions about permissions
can be submitted by email to
thomsonrights@thomson.com.

For more information
contact South-Western,
5191 Natorp Boulevard,
Mason, Ohio, 45040.
Or you can visit our Internet site at:
http://www.swlearning.com

Contemporary Economics

Workbook

Contents

UNIT 5   PUBLIC POLICY AND THE NATIONAL ECONOMY

UNIT 6   THE INTERNATIONAL ECONOMY

Lesson **1.1** The Economic Problem

Part 1—True or False

Directions: Place a *T* for True or an *F* for False in the Answers column to show whether each of the following statements is true or false.

Answers

1. Labor is a type of human resource.   1._____

2. Goods and services are scarce.   2._____

3. A good is free if it involves no apparent cost to you.   3._____

4. Tutoring is an example of a service, not a good.   4._____

5. A bus station is an example of a capital good.   5._____

6. An exhaustible resource can be drawn upon indefinitely, as long as it is used wisely.   6._____

7. Productive resources are defined as the inputs used to produce the goods and services that people want.   7._____

8. The majority of young people in the United States believe that they will likely become wealthy.   8._____

9. A productive resource may only be considered scarce if its price is greater than zero dollars.   9._____

10. Depending on the situation, an entrepreneur does not always need to assume the risk of success or failure in a business venture.   10._____

Part 2—Multiple Choice

Directions: In the Answers column, write the letter that represents the word, or group of words, that correctly completes the statement or answers the question.

Answers

11. Which of the following accurately defines economics? (a) The study of how people make money. (b) The study of seeking profits and increasing resources. (c) The study of the entrepreneur and his or her tactics. (d) The study of how people use scarce resources to satisfy unlimited wants.   11._____

12. Which of the following statements correctly defines the term entrepreneur? (a) a person who tries to earn a profit (b) a person who develops a new product (c) a person who improves an existing product (d) all of the previous   12._____

13. Which of the following type of goods is not a subject of economics? (a) the unemployment rate (b) the stock market (c) anything that is free (d) the shoe industry   13._____

14. Which of the following is a good? (a) dry cleaning (b) deli meat (c) getting a ride from a taxi (d) advertising   14._____

15. Which of the following is a service? (a) writing (b) pens (c) paper (d) computer   15._____

16. Which of the following is a renewable resource, if handled properly? (a) wildlife (b) oil (c) copper ore (d) coal   16._____

17. Which of the following is **not** considered a productive resource? (a) human resources (b) unnatural resources (c) natural resources (d) capital resources   17._____

18. ___?___ is a natural resource. (a) labor (b) factories (c) water (d) trucks   18._____

19. Which of the following is an example of a capital good? (a) rainwater (b) a screwdriver   19._____
    (c) coal (d) a cow

20. Which of the following statements best describes the economic problem? (a) Too many   20._____
    countries are still poor and need more productive resources. (b) We have not discovered how
    to utilize all the productive resources available to us. (c) The productive resources needed to
    satisfy our unlimited wants are too scarce to do so. (d) none of the previous

Part 3—Short Answer

Directions: Read the following questions, and write your response.

21. How does the scarcity of your time affect your study/homework habits?

22. Provide an example of an entrepreneur who introduced a new product or found a better way to produce an existing one.

Part 4—Critical Thinking

Directions: Read the following questions, and write your response.

23. Choose a food product from your kitchen pantry (cereal box, soup can, bag of chips). Examine the package and ingredient list. Discuss how each of the productive resources (factors of production) was involved in the production of the product.

Lesson ⬤1.2 Economic Theory

Part 1—True or False

Directions: Place a *T* for True or an *F* for False in the Answers column to show whether each of the following statements is true or false.

Answers

1. In order to be accurate, theories should be detailed in nature.   1._____

2. According to the circular-flow model, the flows of resources and products are supported by   2._____
   the flows of income and expenditure.

3. Although it is assumed that people are driven by rational self-interest, this does not mean   3._____
   that people are not concerned for others.

4. Making rational consumer choices can be done without time and information.   4._____

5. In the context of economics, marginal is defined as incremental or additional.   5._____

6. All circular-flow models focus on interactions between households and firms.   6._____

7. Households both demand services and supply resources in the economy.   7._____

8. Market economics might focus on the shoe industry.   8._____

9. Economists agree on most theoretical principles based on positive economic analysis.   9._____

10. Economic theories are directly responsible for causing future economic trends.   10._____

Part 2—Multiple Choice

Directions: In the Answers column, write the letter that represents the word, or group of words, that correctly completes the statement or answers the question.

Answers

11. A rational decision maker will change the status quo when the following condition occurs: 11._____
    (a) The expected marginal cost from the change exceeds the expected marginal benefit.
    (b) The expected marginal benefit from the change exceeds the expected marginal cost.
    (c) The expected marginal benefit from the change equals the expected marginal cost.
    (d) none of the previous.

12. Which of the following is a positive economic statement? (a) The economy should experience   12._____
    a recession by next year. (b) The United States experienced its sharpest decrease in
    unemployment last year. (c) More jobs should be created as a result of this administration's
    plans. (d) The recession must be over by the end of this year.

13. Which of the following would be a concern for microeconomists? (a) how the recession   13._____
    affected the unemployment rate (b) how the stock market behaved during the last quarter
    (c) how many people were hired throughout the country last year (d) how a baby boom
    affected the number of diapers sold during the past year

14. Which of the following is **not** an example of a market? (a) a nuclear plant (b) the mall   14._____
    (c) help-wanted ads (d) the Internet

15. According to the circular-flow model, firms do which of the following things? (a) supply   15._____
    goods and services to households (b) demand human resources from households (c) demand
    capital goods through resource markets (d) all of the previous

16. Consumer goods and services are bought in which of the following markets? (a) goods markets (b) service markets (c) product markets (d) resource markets   16._____

17. Which of the following would be a concern for macroeconomists? (a) how the U.S. economy fared during 2004 (b) how Toyota car sales were affected by a recession (c) how many nonfiction books were published last year (d) how higher interest rates affected the ABC Home Construction Company   17._____

18. Which of the following is a normative economic statement? (a) Interest rates were raised twice last year. (b) Cookies in the Jar, a fairly new baking company, nearly doubled its sales this year as compared to last year. (c) The largest grocery store chains should begin hiring more workers because the economy has improved. (d) The price of gasoline increased by 3 cents since yesterday afternoon.   18._____

19. Which of the following is **not** a participant in the economy? (a) firms (b) government (c) households (d) all of the previous participate in the economy   19._____

20. Which of the following is necessary in developing an economic theory? (a) simplify the problem (b) never assume that people make rational choices concerning their self-interests (c) assume that all factors are variables and change constantly (d) all of the previous   20._____

Part 3—Short Answer

Directions: Read the following questions, and write your response.

21. Describe an exchange between your family and a particular business. (The product market)

22. Describe an exchange between a firm and your family. (The resource market)

Part 4—Critical Thinking

23. Following is a cost-benefit analysis of a decision: (A) Attend state college or (B) Attend out-of state college

Create two cost-benefit grids to analyze a decision you have to make. Assign weights to each quadrant based on how important each cost or benefit is to you (1 being not important, 5 being very important). Add your columns and analyze your results. Does this help you with your decision? Explain.

A Attend state college		B Attend out-of-state college	
Costs	**Benefits**	**Cost**	**Benefits**
Parents will visit	Friends attending	$6K more in tuition	No friends attending
Must live in dorm	Can get into program of choice	No campus sports teams	Can live in an apartment
No car	Big campus life	General studies	May have a car

Lesson ●1.3 Opportunity Cost and Choice

Part 1—True or False

Directions: Place a *T* for True or an *F* for False in the Answers column to show whether each of the following statements is true or false.

Answers

1. Because acquiring information about alternatives is costly and time-consuming, you usually make choices based on limited or even faulty information. 1._____

2. According to recent studies, the number of female corporate officers at Fortune 500 companies has decreased over the past two years. 2._____

3. Sunk costs should be carefully considered when making economic decisions. 3._____

4. With every choice comes an opportunity cost. 4._____

5. Opportunity costs are always measured in dollar amounts. 5._____

6. Even a person with unlimited wealth must deal with opportunity costs. 6._____

7. People make decisions based upon the expected opportunity cost of a choice. 7._____

8. Once the opportunity cost of attending college is calculated, it is clear that it is more useful for every young person to go to college instead of entering the work force. 8._____

9. Sunk costs are usually small and they don't affect personal financial status a lot. 9._____

10. It is not wise to spend your time and effort figuring out how to avoid sunk costs. 10._____

Part 2—Multiple Choice

Directions: In the Answers column, write the letter that represents the word, or group of words, that correctly completes the statement or answers the question.

Answers

11. In deciding if you want to attend college, which of these may involve an opportunity cost? (a) value of goods and services that could be purchased with money spent on books (b) value of goods and services that may be purchased with tuition money (c) value of goods and services that may be purchased with money spent on boarding (d) all of the previous 11._____

12. If you must stay at home and study for an upcoming economics test, the opportunity cost of studying would most likely be highest at which of the following times? (a) Monday evening (b) Wednesday morning (c) Thursday afternoon (d) Friday evening 12._____

13. Which of the following statements is true of opportunity costs? (a) It is the value of all alternatives you pass up when you make a choice. (b) It is the value of the best alternative you give up when you make a choice. (c) It can only be measured in dollar terms. (d) It is the same for all individuals. 13._____

14. Economists assume that which of the following leads the average person to choose the most valued alternative among a number of possibilities? (a) rational self-interest (b) scarcity (c) opportunity cost (d) none of the previous 14._____

15. Which of the following would lead to a sunk cost? (a) buying a new CD at an outlet store (b) putting a non-refundable deposit at one college and then attending another (c) deciding to study on a Friday night instead of going to a party (d) none of the previous 15._____

16. If you decide to attend a concert instead of babysitting, which of the following did you need to consider? (a) opportunity cost (b) sunk cost (c) scarcity (d) economic theory 16._____

17. Which of the following is an example of a sunk cost? (a) exchanging one brand of tomato sauce for another one at the grocery store (b) ordering dessert at a restaurant even though 17._____

you're full (c) throwing away the Sunday newspaper before you've read it because your cat tore it to pieces (d) all of the previous

18. Which of the following describes a sunk cost? (a) sunk costs can't be recovered (b) sunk costs have already been incurred (c) sunk costs are irrelevant (d) all of the previous   18._____

19. In the seventeenth century, why did many glassmakers in England refuse to relocate to Virginia? (a) The opportunity cost of doing so was too high. (b) The opportunity cost of doing so was too low. (c) There was no opportunity cost involved. (d) none of the previous   19._____

20. What is considered the ultimate limiting factor in making choices? (a) wealth (b) knowledge (c) time (d) location   20._____

Part 3—Short Answer

Directions: Read the following questions, and write your response.

21. Why do we seldom know the actual opportunity cost of our decisions?

22. Why did Tiger Woods (and some singers and actors) decide that their opportunity cost for attending college was too high?

23. Describe your direct cost and your opportunity cost regarding your decision of what (and where) to have lunch today.

Part 4—Critical Thinking

Directions: Read the following questions and write several sentences in response.

24. Describe your opportunity cost of choosing to attend college next year.

25. Describe your opportunity cost of choosing not to attend college next year.

26. Why is room and board not necessarily an opportunity cost of college?

27. Provide an example of a sunk cost that you have experienced.

Name _____ Class _____ Date _____

Chapter Review

Part 1—True or False

Directions: Place a *T* for True or an *F* for False in the Answers column to show whether each of the following statements is true or false.

Answers

1. Productive resources include human resources and capital resources.   1._____

2. Getting a manicure is an example of a good, not a service.   2._____

3. A tree is an example of a capital resource.   3._____

4. The problem of scarce resources but unlimited wants exists only for the poor.   4._____

5. Future economic trends are not influenced by economic theories.   5._____

6. An exhaustible resource can easily be used up.   6._____

7. Economic decision makers need not consider all costs that are related to their choice.   7._____

8. Time and information are essential to making rational consumer choices.   8._____

9. Market economics might focus on the breakfast cereal industry.   9._____

10. There is no such thing as a truly free good.   10._____

Part 2—Multiple Choice

Directions: In the Answers column, write the letter that represents the word, or group of words, that correctly completes the statement or answers the question.

Answers

11. Which of the following is a positive economic statement? (a) The number of people in the   11._____
workforce increased last year. (b) Unemployment should decrease next year. (c) A war in the
Middle East should jumpstart the economy. (b) all of the previous

12. Which scenario would lead to a sunk cost? (a) going out on a weekend instead of doing your   12._____
homework (b) waiting in one line at the movies and then switching lines when a new window
opens (c) getting a job that pays minimum wage (d) investing in the stock market

13. Which of the following is a scarce resource? (a) the amount of radios sold in the United   13._____
States (b) the radio waves transmitted into the atmosphere (c) the labor needed to produce
radios (d) all of the previous

14. Which of the following is an example of a capital good? (a) cattle (b) a saw (c) a celery stalk   14._____
(d) a television set

15. Which of the following would macroeconomists study? (a) how the stock market affected   15._____
U.S. unemployment rates last year (b) how an increase in the interest rate affected investment
last quarter (c) how a war impacts the unemployment rate (d) all of the previous

16. What do economic theories do? (a) determine how the economy will behave in the year to   16._____
come (b) influence how goods and services are produced (c) make predictions about the
economy (d) completely explain in detail why certain trends occur

17. If you decide to study for an upcoming test instead of going to the movies, what must you   17._____
take into account? (a) sunk cost (b) economic theory (c) opportunity cost (d) scarcity

18. Which of the following is an example of a market? (a) a craft fair (b) a house (c) a tax   18.____
preparation business (d) none of the previous   .

19. What drives people to make economic decisions? (a) concern for the environment (b) rational   19.____
self-interest (c) concerns about scarcity (d) the economic problems of other countries

20. Firms do which of the following things, according to the circular-flow model? (a) supply   20.____
human resources to households (b) demand capital goods (c) are supplied with consumer
goods from households (d) all of the previous

Part 3—Short Answer

Directions: Read the following questions, and write your response.

21. Of the four market participants, into which category or categories do you fall? Explain why.

22. Describe a situation you have experienced that resulted in a sunk cost.

Part 4—Critical Thinking

23. Suppose you would like to open a boutique that sells high-end clothing. You must use a number of
productive resources to get your business started. Provide specific examples of the things you would need
from each of the three productive resource categories. Provide at least one example for each category.

Lesson ⬤2.1 Economic Questions and Economic Systems

Part 1—True or False

Directions: Place a *T* for True or an *F* for False in the Answers column to show whether each of the following statements is true or false.

Answers

1. Traditional economies are based primarily on custom and/or religion. 1._____

2. The three economic questions are completely independent of one another. 2._____

3. In centrally planned economies, the government owns labor. 3._____

4. The number of countries with centrally planned economies who are beginning to embrace the market economy has increased in recent years. 4._____

5. Centrally planned economies assure that no resources are wasted. 5._____

6. Pure centrally planned economies can result in rationed goods. 6._____

7. Markets play a relatively small role in the U.S. economy. 7._____

8. In a pure market economy it may be difficult to enforce property rights. 8._____

9. Citizens of countries with traditional economies are less likely to experience discrimination than citizens of countries with market economies. 9._____

10. Centrally planned economies cause a great deal of environmental damage. 10._____

Part 2—Multiple Choice

Directions: In the Answers column, write the letter that represents the word, or group of words, that correctly completes the statement or answers the question.

Answers

11. In which of these economies might monopolies be possible? (a) pure market economy (b) pure centrally planned economy (c) traditional economy (d) none of the previous 11._____

12. Pure market economies **do not** involve (a) households (b) government (c) firms (d) factories. 12._____

13. ___?___ enjoy(s) the most control in a pure centrally planned economy. (a) the government (b) the wealthy (c) independently owned businesses (d) no one entity 13._____

14. The United States is considered to be a ___?___. (a) pure market economy (b) market economy (c) centrally planned economy (d) transitional economy 14._____

15. Which question does an economy **not** have to answer? (a) How will goods and services be produced? (b) How many goods and services will be produced? (c) What goods and services will be produced? (d) For whom will goods and services be produced? 15._____

16. A pure market economy will most benefit a (a) high-school dropout (b) single mother (c) disabled veteran (d) middle class business woman 16._____

17. Which of the following allows consumers the most choice? (a) centrally planned economy (b) transitional economy (c) pure market economy (d) traditional economy 17._____

18. Which of these countries has a pure market economy? (a) Canada (b) China (c) Australia (d) none of the previous 18._____

19. Ideally, which of these people would a pure centrally planned economy benefit most? (a) the wealthy (b) government officials (c) the most highly educated people (d) the general public   19._____

20. In a pure market economy, which of these factors answers the three economic questions of the economy? (a) the government (b) culture (c) markets (d) all of the previous   20._____

Part 3—Short Answer

Directions: Read the following questions, and write your response.

21. Who coordinates the activities of the market place?

22. What does Adam Smith's metaphor of the "invisible hand" illustrate?

23. Why have so many centrally planned economies allowed a greater role for private ownership and market competition?

Part 4—Critical Thinking

Directions: Examine the problems of a pure market economy described in the text. Using your knowledge of the United States, a mixed economy with a strong market system, give an example relating to how the following problems are dealt with in the United States.

24. Difficulty enforcing property rights.

25. Some people have few resources to sell.

26. Some firms try to monopolize markets.

27. No public goods.

Lesson ⬤ 2.2 Production Possibilities Frontier

Part 1—True or False

Directions: Place a *T* for True or an *F* for False in the Answers column to show whether each of the following statements is true or false.

Answers

1. The resources in the economy are not all perfectly adaptable to the production of both consumer and capital goods.   1._____

2. Changes in technology do not usually affect production.   2._____

3. The law of increasing opportunity cost states that each additional increment of one good requires the economy to give up successively larger increments of the other good.   3._____

4. Producing more capital goods during a particular period is likely to shift the economy's PPF outward the next period.   4._____

5. Efficiency is producing the maximum possible output from available resources.   5._____

6. Upward movement along the PPF involves giving up some of one good to get more of another.   6._____

7. The PPF model illustrates the production of goods but not services.   7._____

8. If many workers decided to retire at an earlier age, the PPF would shift inward.   8._____

9. Movement down the PPF curve indicates that the opportunity cost of more capital goods is more consumer goods.   9._____

10. The PPF demonstrates that choice is an essential part of an economy.   10._____

Part 2—Multiple Choice

Directions: In the Answers column, write the letter that represents the word, or group of words, that correctly completes the statement or answers the question.

Answers

11. What purpose does the production possibilities frontier (PPF) serve? (a) It determines whether the economy is expanding or experiencing a recession. (b) It predicts the possible outcomes of a rise in unemployment. (c) It proves that while the production of some goods increases the efficiency of the economy, the production of others decreases the efficiency. (d) It shows the possible combinations of goods that can be produced when available resources are employed fully and efficiently.   11._____

12. What do points outside of the PPF indicate? (a) unattainable combinations of goods (b) ideal combinations of goods (c) inefficient combinations of goods (d) none of the previous   12._____

13. Economic growth effects the PPF by (a) shifting it inward (b) shifting it outward (c) causing no change at all (d) turning it into a straight line.   13._____

14. Suppose that during a given period an economy produces a large amount of capital goods. What would you expect to happen to the amount of output produced during the following period? (a) Less output would be produced. (b) More output would be produced. (c) Output would not be affected. (d) none of the previous   14._____

15. Which of the following is not one of the PPF model's assumptions? (a) The model focuses on production during a given period. (b) The resources available in the economy are fixed in quantity and quality. (c) The model focuses only on consumer goods. (d) Available technology does not change during a given time period.   15._____

16. Suppose that a new machine that speeds up automobile production is introduced into the auto industry. This would cause the PPF to (a) shift outward (b) shift inward (c) do nothing (d) Not enough information is given.   16._____

17. What do points inside the PPF indicate? (a) the combination of goods that employ resources efficiently (b) combinations of goods that employ resources fully (c) the combination of goods that do not employ resources fully (d) none of the previous   17._____

18. Which of the following situations might cause an inward shift in the production possibilities frontier (PPF)? (a) A computer network shuts down due to a virus. (b) More people earn bachelor degrees. (c) A new machine that produces bread faster is invented. (d) OPEC announces a new source of oil.   18._____

19. An increase in the labor force would cause the PPF to (a) shift inward (b) shift outward (c) do nothing (d) turn into a straight line   19._____

20. The PPF bows outward. Which of the following concepts does this illustrate? (a) the law of increasing scarcity (b) the law of economic growth (c) the law of decreasing efficiency (d) the law of increasing opportunity cost   20._____

Part 3—Short Answer

Directions: Read the following questions, and write your response.

21. How does the production possibilities frontier (PPF) illustrate efficiency?

22. What accounts for the shape of the PPF?

Part 4—Critical Thinking

Directions: Construct a production possibilities frontier that indicates efficient use of resources to be 6 million in production of consumer goods and 8 million in production of capital goods.

23. Suppose that over time, a new technology enables resources to perform in a new way that benefits the production of consumer goods only. Indicate the new curve on your graph as point A.

24. Suppose that over time, a new resource is discovered that increases production of capital goods only. Indicate the new curve on your graph as point B.

Lesson (2.3) Comparative Advantage

Part 1—True or False

Directions: Place a *T* for True or an *F* for False in the Answers column to show whether each of the following statements is true or false.

Answers

1. Sometimes it is vital to allocate resources across the country to reach efficiency.   1._____

2. According to the law of comparative advantage, the worker with the higher opportunity cost of producing a particular output should specialize in that output.   2._____

3. Absolute advantage is the best way to decide who should perform a particular task.   3._____

4. If a firm employs one person to answer telephone calls and another to reply to email messages, the firm is applying the concept of specialization.   4._____

5. Money is the most accepted system of exchange throughout the world.   5._____

6. Specialization is the ideal way to run a business as there are no disadvantages to it.   6._____

7. If you exchange money for a hamburger, you are engaging in bartering.   7._____

8. It is more efficient for the United States to import coconuts from another country than to try and grow coconuts within the country.   8._____

9. Using specialization in an economy increases efficiency.   9._____

10. The benefits gained from specialization result only from systems containing individuals and small firms, not those containing large regions or whole countries.   10._____

Part 2—Multiple Choice

Directions: In the Answers column, write the letter that represents the word, or group of words, that correctly completes the statement or answers the question.

Answers

11. Suppose three firms—Donut World, Donut Mania, and Lotta Donuts—all produce donuts. Given the same resources, Donut World can produce 10,000 donuts per day, Donut Mania produces 15,000 donuts per day, and Lotta Donuts produces 8,000 donuts per day. Which firm has the absolute advantage? (a) Donut World (b) Donut Mania (c) Lotta Donuts (d) It cannot be determined from the information given   11._____

12. Which of the following focuses on which given firm uses the fewest resources to produce goods? (a) comparative advantage (b) division of labor (c) absolute advantage (d) none of the previous   12._____

13. Which of the following situations reflects specialization? (a) A factory worker is responsible for installing a belt on a vacuum cleaner that is being manufactured. (b) A veterinarian advertises that he can treat any type of animal. (c) A writer both edits and markets her own book. (d) none of the previous   13._____

14. Which of the following terms focuses on the opportunity cost of resources used in producing a given product? (a) comparative advantage (b) division of labor (c) absolute advantage (d) none of the previous   14._____

15. Which of these economies would benefit most from a barter system? (a) United States (b) a large European city (c) small island community in the Caribbean (d) all of the previous   15._____

16. Which of the following situations does **not** reflect division of labor? (a) A restaurant employs servers, cooks, and bus boys. (b) A school hires a Spanish teacher and a gym teacher to fill its vacancies. (c) As a gift for a bride, each family member makes one patch of a large quilt. (d) An accountant acts as her own secretary.   16._____

17. Which of the following should be first and foremost taken into account when determining who should specialize in what? (a) absolute advantage (b) comparative advantage (c) the bartering system (d) none of the previous   17._____

18. How does division of labor increase productivity? (a) Workers can improve their skills through repetition. (b) It allows the use of sophisticated production techniques. (c) Workers are happier because they can do the tasks they prefer. (a) all of the previous   18._____

19. Suppose Bob can change the oil in his car more quickly than Evan can. Which of the following does Bob have? (a) opportunity cost (b) division of labor (c) specialization (d) absolute advantage   19._____

20. Tina wants a new pair of tennis shoes, so she goes to the local department store and pay $30 in cash for a new pair. Which type of exchange has Tina employed? (a) barter (b) money (c) credit (d) loan   20._____

Part 3—Critical Thinking

Directions: Analyze the potential trade situation between the countries of Bulgaria and Macedonia. Both countries use their fertile land to produce grapes or to raise chickens. Analyze the production capabilities depicted in the chart below.

	Bulgaria	Macedonia
Grapes	400 units	300 units
Chickens	200 units	100 units

		Answers			Answers
21.	Which country has the absolute advantage for producing grapes?		26.	Determine the opportunity cost for producing another unit of chickens in Macedonia.	
22.	Which country has the absolute advantage for producing chickens?		27.	The comparative advantage belongs to the producer with the lower opportunity cost for producing the identical good or service. Which country has the comparative advantage for producing grapes and which has the comparative advantage for producing chickens?	
23.	Determine the opportunity cost for producing another unit of grapes in Bulgaria.				
24.	Determine the opportunity cost for producing another unit of grapes in Macedonia.				
25.	Determine the opportunity cost for producing another unit of chickens in Bulgaria.				

Chapter ❷ Review

Part 1—True or False

Directions: Place a *T* for True or an *F* for False in the Answers column to show whether each of the following statements is true or false.

Answers

1. If a bakery hires one person to bake cookies and another to bake cakes, the bakery is applying the concept of specialization.   1._____

2. An economy's production possibility frontier will shift inward if more capital goods are produced during a period of time.   2._____

3. Bartering is defined as exchanging goods for money.   3._____

4. Countries with traditional economies are usually the most advanced.   4._____

5. Centrally planned economies are less likely to do damage to the environment than market economies.   5._____

6. Absolute advantage should not be the only factor considered when dividing labor.   6._____

7. Points along a production possibilities frontier identify the numerous points at which an economy's resources are used inefficiently.   7._____

8. Markets play a large part in the U.S. economy.   8._____

9. An economy that utilizes specialization is more efficient than one that does not.   9._____

10. Today, there are no more centrally planned economies.   10._____

Part 2—Multiple Choice

Directions: In the Answers column, write the letter that represents the word, or group of words, that correctly completes the statement or answers the question.

Answers

11. Which of the following people would a pure market economy benefit least? (a) the CEO of a major corporation (b) an unemployed engineer (c) a stock broker (d) a caterer   11._____

12. Suppose Connie can knit 3 scarves a week, Abigail can knit 5 scarves a week and Mary can knit 2 scarves a week. Who has the absolute advantage? (a) Connie (b) Abigail (c) Mary (d) It cannot be determined from the information given.   12._____

13. Points inside the production possibilities frontier indicate (a) inefficient combinations of goods (b) unattainable combinations of goods (c) ideal combinations of goods (d) none of the previous   13._____

14. A production possibilities frontier will shift outward if (a) advances in technology take place (b) the amount of workers decreases (c) people invest less money (d) all of the previous   14._____

15. Suppose Bobby exchanges his Mickey Mantel baseball card for a Pete Rose baseball card. What has Bobby engaged in? (a) loan (b) monetary exchange (c) bartering (d) crediting   15._____

16. How does division of labor affect productivity? (a) It increases productivity. (b) It decreases productivity. (c) It does not affect productivity. (d) none of the previous   16._____

17. Which of the following is the best example of a division of labor? (a) Linda buys groceries while Tina studies. (b) Linda tutors Tina while Tina pays Linda for her time. (c) Linda reads the newspaper while Tina reads a magazine. (d) Linda builds airplane models while Tina paints them.   17._____

18. The government has the most power in which of these economies? (a) pure market economy (b) transitional economy (c) market economy (d) centrally planned economy   18._____

19. What does the production possibilities frontier assume? (a) Services, but not goods, are taken into account. (b) Technology remains constant. (c) The resources in an economy are always changing. (d) There is no specific period of time given.   19._____

20. What are transitional economies? (a) economies that are in the process of shifting orientation from central planning to competitive markets (b) economies that deal exclusively with the barter system (c) economies that are in the process of shifting orientation from competitive markets to central planning (d) economies that deal exclusively with cash exchanges   20._____

Part 3— Critical Thinking

21. Imagine you are the president of a new country. You are trying to decide which type of economy would be best for your citizens. Fill in the chart below to help you visualize the advantages and disadvantages of each economy. Then, based on your answers, explain which type of economy is best for your country and why.

	Pure Centrally Planned Economy	Pure Market Economy	Mixed Economy
Advantages			
Disadvantages			

Lesson (3.1) The U.S. Private Sector

Part 1—True or False

Directions: Place a *T* for True or an *F* for False in the Answers column to show whether each of the following statements is true or false.

Answers

1. Foreign economies can have a significant effect on the U.S. economy. 1._____

2. International trade between the United States and the rest of the world has decreased in recent decades. 2._____

3. The number of women working outside the home has grown during the last century. 3._____

4. The Industrial Revolution was so successful that there is no longer a need for farmers. 4._____

5. Less production now occurs in the home and more goods and services are purchased in markets as compared to 100 years ago. 5._____

6. Less than 1 percent of the U.S. labor force works in the agricultural industry. 6._____

7. The household is the most important economic decision maker. 7._____

8. Although much of the population worked on farms in 1850, there was no specialization within the farm structure. 8._____

9. Throughout the years, households have become increasingly self-sufficient. 9._____

10. The number of two-earner households has steadily decreased over the past 100 years. 10._____

Part 2—Multiple Choice

Directions: In the Answers column, write the letter that represents the word, or group of words, that correctly completes the statement or answers the question.

Answers

11. In the last half of the nineteenth century many farmers gave up farming to move to cities because (a) fewer farmers were needed due to agricultural advances (b) urban factories needed workers (c) the economy focused less on agriculture (d) all of the previous 11._____

12. Which of the following best illustrates the cottage industry system? (a) Two small firms merge together and create electronic equipment. (b) Household members make potholders and sell them. (c) A factory provides a household with cloth which members use to produce shirts. (d) A student hires a tutor for help with Algebra. 12._____

13. Which of the following choices would maximize the utility of a household? (a) A household allows weeds to grow in the driveway. (b) A household that repairs a leaky basement. (c) Members of a household refuse to replace old, inefficient windows with new ones. (d) Although a house is infested with rodents, an exterminator is not called. 13._____

14. Which of the following products does the United States produce more of than it needs? (a) wheat (b) oil (c) aluminum (d) copper 14._____

15. Which of the following best defines the term "firm"? (a) the most important economic decision maker consisting of all those living under one roof (b) economic unit formed by an entrepreneur who combines resources to produce goods and services and accepts risk of profit and loss (c) organization that solicits funds to help the poor (d) none of the previous 15._____

16. Which of the following statements about the cottage industry is most accurate?   16._____
(a) Over the years, production evolved from factories that produce most goods under one roof to the cottage industry system to self-sufficient rural households. (b) Over the years, production evolved from self-sufficient rural households to the cottage industry system to factories that produce most goods under one roof. (c) Over the years, production evolved from the cottage industry system to factories that produce most goods under one roof to self-sufficient rural households. (d) none of the previous.

17. Which of the following was associated with the Industrial Revolution? (a) technological   17._____
developments increased (b) the popularity of the cottage industry increased (c) there was an increase in rural farms (d) Great Britain benefited greatly from it, but the Industrial Revolution never spread to other countries

18. What do firms accomplish that self-sufficient households cannot? (a) Firms produce goods   18._____
that are superior to those produced in self-sufficient households. (b) Firms are able to pay those who produce goods more money than households can. (c) Firms are able to reduce transaction costs for each good. (d) all of the previous

19. Which of the following was **not** a feature of the factories that surfaced during the Industrial   19._____
Revolution? (a) Production was directly supervised. (b) Division of labor was more efficient. (c) Large, specialized machines were used. (d) Transportation costs increased.

20. Suppose that you own an ice cream shop. The cost of producing one pint of ice cream is   20._____
$2.50. The revenue earned is $3.75. What is your profit per ice cream pint? (a) $.25 (b) $1.00 (c) $1.25 (d) $6.25

Part 3—Critical Thinking

Directions: Read the following questions, and write several sentences in response.

21. Consider the household that you live in. Describe the economic choices that are made by your household on a daily basis. (These choices include what to buy, how much to save, where to live and where to work).

22. How does your household maximize utility? (How does it reach household goals?)

23. How does your household gain from specialization and comparative advantage? (What is produced, what is not produced yet paid to a specialist to produce?)

Lesson ⬤3.2 Regulating the Private Sector

Part 1—True or False

Directions: Place a *T* for True or an *F* for False in the Answers column to show whether each of the following statements is true or false.

Answers

1. Most businesspeople would prefer to be monopolists—that is, to be the only seller of a product.   1._____

2. Monetary policy helps to control fluctuations in the economy through taxation and public spending.   2._____

3. The government tests firms' standards of measurements to ensure that the consumer is getting what he or she is paying for.   3._____

4. Monopolies may harm other businesses, but they rarely damage social welfare.   4._____

5. Public utilities are government-owned and government-regulated monopolies.   5._____

6. Private property rights don't allow owners to do what they want with their property.   6._____

7. Only the federal government can influence fiscal policy.   7._____

8. The government may protect both private and intellectual property.   8._____

9. Competition in a particular market promotes lower prices.   9._____

10. Some monopolies are beneficial.   10._____

Part 2—Multiple Choice

Directions: In the Answers column, write the letter that represents the word, or group of words, that correctly completes the statement or answers the question.

Answers

11. A good example of a trademark would be (a) Toni Morrison's next novel (b) a painting by Picasso (c) Target's red target symbol (d) none of the previous   11._____

12. The government safeguards private property through (a) legal contracts (b) national defense (c) policies (d) all of the previous   12._____

13. To combat rising inflation the government could (a) increase taxes (b) increase government spending (c) increase the amount of money in circulation (d) all of the previous   13._____

14. Which of the following regulates the safety of over-the-counter drugs? (a) the U.S. Department of Agriculture (b) the U.S. Food and Drug Administration (c) the Consumer Product Safety Commission (d) the U.S. Bureau of Weights and Measures   14._____

15. Which of the following regulates monetary policy? (a) the Consumer Product Safety Commission (b) the U.S. Department of Monetary Regulation (c) the Federal Reserve System. (d) the U.S. Bureau of Weights and Measures   15._____

16. To decrease its spending the government would enact which of the following policies? (a) inflation (b) monetary (c) fiscal (d) monopoly   16._____

17. Which of the following things do antitrust laws accomplish? (a) encourage the creation of monopolies (b) influence the political system (c) discourage competition within the market (d) reduce anticompetitive behavior   17._____

18. Suppose that a number of companies that produce cars join together, making it difficult for other firms to compete. Which of the following could prevent such a situation? (a) monetary policy (b) antitrust laws (c) fiscal policy (d) private property rights   18._____

19. Which of the following is associated with innovation? (a) A scientist who invents a new way to launder clothing works with a firm to make his product marketable. (b) The inventor of a new type of running shoe applies for a patent. (c) The owner of a dry-cleaning business discovers a new way of organizing his shop. (d) all of the previous   19._____

20. Which of the following reflects the rise and fall of economic activity relative to the long-term growth trend of the economy? (a) natural monopolies (b) monetary policy (c) business cycles (d) fiscal policy   20._____

Part 3—Short Answer

Directions: Read the following questions and write several sentences in response.

21. Many economists suggest that increased support of private property rights is the single most important factor in raising the standard of living in developing countries throughout the world. Why are private property rights so important?

22. What role do governments play in promoting private property?

23. What is the function of the U.S. Bureau of Weights and Measures?

Part 4—Critical Thinking

Directions: Read the following questions and write several sentences in response.

24. Illustrate a familiar trademark (other than the Nike swoosh and McDonald's arches).

25. If a firm's goal is to maximize profit, why is it punished if it achieves monopoly power?

26. Fiscal and monetary policy both are used to help stabilize the business cycle. How do the approaches of these policies differ?

Lesson (3.3) Public Goods and Externalities

Part 1—True or False

Directions: Place a *T* for True or an *F* for False in the Answers column to show whether each of the following statements is true or false.

Answers

1. Encouraging education is one way the government tries to attain positive externalities.   1._____

2. The government usually regulates open-access goods.   2._____

3. Nonpayers are easily excluded from public goods.   3._____

4. Fish is an example of a quasi-public good.   4._____

5. It is costly to exclude people from open-access goods.   5._____

6. The quality and quantity of an open-access resource tends to deteriorate over time.   6._____

7. Overall, the private sector, operating on its own, produces more negative externalities than positive externalities.   7._____

8. An example of a positive externality is training others to teach illiterate adults to read.   8._____

9. Zoning laws try to reduce positive externalities.   9._____

10. Education leads to negative externalities.   10._____

Part 2—Multiple Choice

Directions: In the Answers column, write the letter that represents the word, or group of words, that correctly completes the statement or answers the question.

Answers

11. Private goods are always which of the following? (a) nonrival, nonexclusive (b) nonrival, exclusive (c) rival, nonexclusive (d) rival, exclusive   11._____

12. A fast-food meal can be described by which of the following two terms? (a) nonrival, nonexclusive (b) nonrival, exclusive (c) rival, nonexclusive (d) rival, exclusive   12._____

13. Which of the following is a way that the government can correct for negative externalities? (a) The government relaxes local zoning laws. (b) The government increases the legal amount of waste that can be emptied into rivers and streams. (c) The government enacts antipollution laws. (d) all of the previous   13._____

14. Which of the following situations might lead to a positive externality? (a) Your brother decides to go to medical school. (b) A child's mother smokes cigarettes. (c) A new diaper that is not biodegradable is introduced into the market. (d) all of the previous   14._____

15. A deer in a forest that people hunt can be described by which of the following? (a) nonrival, nonexclusive (b) nonrival, exclusive (c) rival, nonexclusive (d) rival, exclusive   15._____

16. Which of the following is an example of a quasi-public good? (a) radio programs (b) an automobile (c) sheep (d) a jar of salsa   16._____

17. Suppose the government passes a law that makes it illegal to hunt foxes without a license. Foxes can now be described as which of the following? (a) exclusive (b) nonexclusive (c) private (d) negative externality   17._____

18. Which of the following is available to all but can be kept from nonpayers? (a) private goods 18._____
(b) open-access goods (c) public goods (d) quasi-public goods

19. Which of the following is an example of an open-access good? (a) potatoes (b) picture frames 19._____
(c) television signals (d) deer

20. Which of the following situations might lead to a negative externality? (a) A large power 20._____
plant disposes of toxic waste in the local river. (b) The introduction of small electric cars
reduces U.S. reliance on imported oil. (c) A non-biodegradable cleaning product becomes
extremely popular with consumers. (d) all of the previous

Part 3—Short Answer

Directions: Read the following questions, and write your response.

21. Explain why forests and salmon-filled rivers are considered to be renewable resources.

22. Explain the differing role of government regarding negative and positive externalities.

23. What are some positive externalities that a high school brings to its community?

Part 4—Critical Thinking

Directions: Read the following questions, and write your response.

24. List some of the negative externalities in your community that result from production or consumption?

25. Suggest remedies or corrections for these existing negative externalities.

Part 5—Organizing

26. **Directions:** Create a chart that categorizes the following goods and services as rival or nonrival, exclusive or nonexclusive.

GOODS AND SERVICES	ANSWER
a school lunch	
a highway	
a Taco Bell burrito	
deer during hunting season	
welfare assistance	
fresh air	

Name _____ Class _____ Date _____

Lesson 3.4   Providing a Safety Net

Part 1—True or False

Directions: Place a *T* for True or an *F* for False in the Answers column to show whether each of the following statements is true or false.

Answers

1. The United States has the lowest rate of teenage pregnancy in the developed world.   1._____

2. An earned-income tax credit benefits the wealthiest 10 percent of the country.   2._____

3. China has a higher official poverty level than the United States.   3._____

4. Some states allow all welfare recipients to remain on welfare for more than five years.   4._____

5. Today, families are not allowed to receive welfare benefits for more than one year.   5._____

6. Overall, people with more education earn more on average.   6._____

7. Supplemental Security Income may help support people addicted to drugs.   7._____

8. The qualifying level of income to be accepted by Medicaid varies by state.   8._____

9. Two-parent families use welfare less often than single-parent families.   9._____

10. Welfare is an example of a social insurance program.   10._____

Part 2—Multiple Choice

Directions: In the Answers column, write the letter that represents the word, or group of words, that correctly completes the statement or answers the question.

Answers

11. Which of the following best describes median income? (a) the income in a group of incomes   11._____
that is most common (b) the average income among a group of incomes (c) the middle
income when a group of incomes is ranked low to high (d) none of the previous

12. Which of the following households is at the greatest risk for living in poverty? (a) single   12._____
fathers (b) married couples who are both present in the home (c) single mothers (d) divorced
couples who share custody of children

13. Which of the following provides health insurance for those with incomes below a certain   13._____
level? (a) Supplemental Security Income (b) Medicaid (c) Temporary Assistance for Needy
Families (d) Medicare

14. Which of the following people would **not** receive social insurance benefits? (a) a single   14._____
teenage mother with no employment history (b) a retired teacher (c) an unemployed
construction worker (d) a factory worker who has been laid off

15. Which of the following is a type of social insurance program? (a) welfare (b) Medicaid   15._____
(c) Supplemental Security Income (d) Social Security

16. Which of the following might be considered a reason why household incomes vary?   16._____
(a) education levels differ (b) mental abilities differ (c) physical abilities differ (d) all of the
previous

17. What happens to the number of people living in poverty during a recession? (a) The number   17._____
    increases. (b) The number decreases. (c) The number is unaffected. (d) none of the previous

18. Which of the following supplements wages of the working poor? (a) the income   18._____
    redistribution program (b) earned-income tax credits (c) Supplemental Security Income (d)
    Medicare

19. Which of the following best defines a means-tested program? (a) advertising how much the   19._____
    government spends on programs to help the poor (b) help in the form of goods and services
    (c) a program that makes up for the lost income of people who worked but are now retired,
    temporarily unemployed, or unable to work because of disability or work-related injury (d) a
    household's income and assets must fall below a certain level to qualify for benefits

20. Which of the following best describes mean income? (a) the income in a group of incomes   20._____
    that is most common (b) the average income among a group of incomes (c) the middle
    income when a group of incomes is ranked low to high (d) none of the previous

Part 3—Short Answer

Directions: Read the following questions and write several sentences in response.

21. How is the official poverty rate determined?

22. How does the "earned-income tax credit" assist the working poor?

23. What other assistance programs are available to the working poor?

Part 4—Critical Thinking

24. **Directions:** Compare and contrast social insurance programs (Social Security and Medicare) and income-
    assistance programs (welfare programs).

Chapter (3) Review

Part 1—True or False

Directions: Place a *T* for True or an *F* for False in the Answers column to show whether each of the following statements is true or false.

Answers

1. Today welfare recipients receive benefits for a shorter period of time than they did in the past.

    1._____

2. The government is the most important economic decision maker.

    2._____

3. It is against the law for the government to run a monopoly.

    3._____

4. Antitrust laws prevent monopolies from developing.

    4._____

5. Wild ducks are an example of an open-access good.

    5._____

6. The number of workers in the agricultural industry in the United States has steadily increased since the Industrial Revolution.

    6._____

7. Earned-income tax credits supplement the wages of the working poor.

    7._____

8. It is the government's responsibility to ensure that gas pumps measure a consumer's gallon of gas accurately.

    8._____

9. A means-tested program is defined as a program that benefits people who are temporarily out of work.

    9._____

10. Divisions of labor became common during the Industrial Revolution.

    10._____

Part 2—Multiple Choice

Directions: In the Answers column, write the letter that represents the word, or group of words, that correctly completes the statement or answers the question.

Answers

11. Which of the following is an example of a positive externality? (a) After graduating from law school, you teach other law students. (b) Your sister donates food to a shelter. (c) Your friend adopts a dog at the local humane society. (d) all of the previous

    11._____

12. What does Medicaid do? (a) provide unemployment insurance (b) provide health insurance for those whose income is below a certain level (c) provide benefits for those who are retired (d) none of the previous

    12._____

13. Which of the following is an example of a quasi-public good? (a) potato chips (b) cattle (c) television programs (d) cotton

    13._____

14. Suppose that you own a burrito shop. The cost of producing one burrito is $4. You earn $6 in revenue. What is your profit per burrito? (a) $1 (b) $4 (c) $6 (d) $2

    14._____

15. Which terms best describe a pair of Gap jeans? (a) rival, exclusive (b) nonrival, exclusive (c) rival, nonexclusive (d) nonrival, nonexclusive.

    15._____

16. Which of the following is not an economic decision maker in the U.S. private sector? (a) firms (b) the rest of the world (c) the government (d) households.

    16._____

17. Which government agency ensures that toys are safe for children? (a) the U.S. Bureau of   17._____
Weights and Measures (b) the U.S. Department of Monetary Regulation (c) the U.S. Food and
Drug Administration (d) the Consumer Product Safety Commission.

18. Suppose that a number of companies that make computers join together, making it difficult   18._____
for other companies to compete. How might the government respond? (a) impose fiscal policy
(b) impose antitrust laws (c) impose monetary policy (d) impose stricter Medicaid guidelines

19. Which of the following best illustrates innovation? (a) a chemist works with a car company to 19._____
create a paint that withstands harsh weather conditions (b) a writer is hired by a law firm to
create consumer pamphlets (c) a scientist studies why the dinosaurs became extinct (d) none
of the previous

20. Which of the following would be considered a trademark? (a) Nike's swoosh (b) McDonald's 20._____
golden arches (c) MGM's roaring lion (d) all of the previous.

Part 3—Short Answer

Directions: Read the following questions and write several sentences in response.

21. You have decided that you'd like to maximize the utility of your household. Describe two ways that you
could accomplish this.

22. Discuss the three rules of a market economy and provide examples of how these rules are enforced.

Part 4—Critical Thinking

23. Suppose you have a friend who was laid off from her job of three years. She is a widow and has two young
children. She's not sure what to do next. What advice would you give her? Specifically, what government
programs could she take advantage of?

Lesson   **4.1**   The Demand Curve

Part 1—True or False

Directions: Place a *T* for True or an *F* for False in the Answers column to show whether each of the following statements is true or false.

Answers

1. Demand curves may appear as straight lines.   1._____

2. The law of diminishing marginal utility affects all consumption.   2._____

3. Quantity demanded is represented by one point on the demand curve, whereas demand is represented by the entire demand curve.   3._____

4. Market demand reflects the demand of an individual consumer.   4._____

5. A demand curve displays quantity demanded on the horizontal axis.   5._____

6. The information in a demand schedule may be expressed graphically in a demand curve.   6._____

7. The law of demand states that quantity demanded varies directly with price, other things constant.   7._____

8. A change in the price of one good relative to changes in the prices of other similar goods can cause the substitution effect.   8._____

9. A decrease in the price of soda affects your real income, not your money income.   9._____

10. The demand for a good is the entire relation between price and quantities demanded.   10._____

Part 2—Multiple Choice

Directions: In the Answers column, write the letter that represents the word, or group of words, that correctly completes the statement or answers the question.

Answers

11. Which of the following is **not** a determinant of demand? (a) price of related goods (b) consumer expectations (c) number of consumers (d) supply   11._____

12. Which of the following directly causes the substitution effect? (a) The public begins to grow tired of certain products. (b) Total utility changes. (c) The price of a good changes in relation to the prices of other similar goods. (d) Advances in technology are made.   12._____

13. Which of the following scenarios reflects the law of diminishing marginal utility? (a) Your friend offers you a second piece of birthday cake, but you reply that you are full. (b) You calculate that each person at a party you are throwing will drink two cans of soda. (c) You take advantage of a fast-food restaurant's promotion and buy two burgers for $2. (d) You are still hungry after eating a salad and order an English muffin.   13._____

14. A demand curve must include which of the following items? (a) how much product is supplied to consumers (b) the type of units being used to measure the product (c) the prices of substitute goods (d) the number of suppliers in the market   14._____

15. Which of the following terms is defined as the demand of a single consumer? (a) quantity demanded (b) the demand curve (c) market demand (d) individual demand   15._____

16. Suppose that your favorite gum decreases in price. Your ___?___ is most affected. (a) money income (b) real income (c) overall income (d) marginal utility   16._____

17. Which of the following situations best illustrates the substitution effect? (a) The price of CDs   17. _____
decreases, and you are able to buy two CDs this week instead of your usual one CD per week.
(b) Laundry detergent is on sale at the grocery store this week, so you purchase five bottles.
(c) You had planned to buy subs for your Super Bowl party, but the price of subs increased so
you instead buy pizzas. (d) all of the previous

18. Suppose an ice cream shop sells cones that can be topped with one, two, or three scoops of ice   18. _____
cream. Each additional scoop increases the overall price of the ice cream cone, so the shop
wants to sell as many scoops as possible. How might the shop owners counteract the law of
diminishing marginal utility? (a) They may decrease the price of each additional ice cream
scoop. (b) They may decrease the amount of flavors that customers are offered. (c) They may
increase the price of the cone itself. (d) all of the previous

19. How is a market demand curve created? (a) The demands of a hand-selected group of   19. _____
consumers are combined. (b) The individual demands of all consumers are averaged. (c) The
demands of Americans are removed from the demands of the rest of the world. (d) The
individual demands of all consumers in the market are combined.

20. Suppose the price of glue increases during a given time period. How will the demand for glue   20. _____
be affected? (a) decreases (b) increases (c) remains constant (d) It cannot be determined from
the information given.

Part 3— Graphing

21. **Directions:** Suppose a student club at your school is having a fresh-baked cookie sale on campus tomorrow.
You and three friends can purchase your favorite cookies as they come out of an oven. Create your
individual demand schedules for these 5-inch round gourmet delights. Determine the quantity demanded for
each of you at price points of $.10, $.50, $1.00, and $1.50 per cookie. Fill out the individual demand
schedule for you and your three friends.

You	Student 1	Student 2	Student 3

22. Compute the market demand (sum of the individual demand schedules). Label and create a demand curve
depicting the market demand for these cookies.

Market Demand

Lesson (4.2) Elasticity of Demand

Part 1—True or False

Directions: Place a *T* for True or an *F* for False in the Answers column to show whether each of the following statements is true or false.

Answers

1. Demand is almost always more elastic at higher prices and less elastic at lower prices.   1._____

2. Economists do not usually differentiate between the short-run and long-run when estimating elasticity.   2._____

3. Elasticity of demand cannot be estimated.   3._____

4. When calculating elasticity you do not need to focus on how output or price is measured.   4._____

5. The longer the adjustment period, the greater the consumers' ability to substitute relatively higher-priced products with lower-priced substitutes.   5._____

6. Demand for cigarettes among teenage smokers is less elastic than that of adult smokers.   6._____

7. Elasticity of demand values are sorted into four categories.   7._____

8. Demand is unit elastic if it is less than 1.0.   8._____

9. Elasticity of demand is greater in the short-run.   9._____

10. If demand is inelastic, producers will never willingly cut the price since doing so would reduce total revenue.   10._____

Part 2—Multiple Choice

Directions: In the Answers column, write the letter that represents the word, or group of words, that correctly completes the statement or answers the question.

Answers

11. Which of the following is a factor in calculating the elasticity of demand? (a) percentage change in quantity supplied (b) percentage change in total revenue (c) percentage change in price (d) none of the previous   11._____

12. Suppose that you have found a shampoo that works wonders for your hair. Nothing else can achieve the same results. What might you assume about that product's elasticity of demand? (a) The shampoo has an extremely high elasticity of demand. (b) The shampoo has an extremely low elasticity of demand. (c) The shampoo has an average elasticity of demand. (d) It cannot be determined from the information given.   12._____

13. Suppose that the elasticity of demand of socks is 0.7. If the price of socks is reduced by 10 percent, how will sales be affected? (a) Sales will grow by more than 10 percent. (b) Sales will grow by less than 10 percent. (c) Sales will grow by 10 percent. (d) Sales will decrease by 10 percent.   13._____

14. Suppose that when paper plates sell for $2 per package, the demand is 5 million. Which of the following is the total revenue earned? (a) $10 million (b) $3 million (c) $7 million (d) $1 million   14._____

15. Suppose the price of envelopes increases from $1.09 per box to $1.50 per box. The quantity demanded decreases from 2 million to 1.5 million. Which of the following is the elasticity of demand? (a) 0.66 (b) 1.0 (c) 1.5 (d) 1.67   15._____

16. Based on your answer for item 15, which of the following describes the elasticity of demand for the envelopes? (a) inelastic (b) elastic (c) unit-elastic (d) all of the previous   16._____

17. Which of the following goods is the most price elastic? (a) toothpicks (b) cat food (c) televisions (d) automobiles   17._____

18. The demand elasticity for cigarettes among teenage smokers is estimated to be 1.3. How would a 7 percent increase in the price of cigarettes affect sales among teenagers? (a) The quantity demanded would fall by less than 7 percent. (b) The quantity demanded would fall by more than 7 percent. (c) The quantity demanded would fall by exactly 7 percent. (d) It cannot be determined from the information given.   18._____

19. Suppose a product's elasticity of demand is 1.7. How responsive is the quantity demanded to a change in price? (a) not responsive (b) relatively responsive (c) negatively responsive (d) It cannot be determined from the information given.   19._____

20. Suppose one group of economists is examining the market for jackets. Another group is examining the market for Stay Warm jackets while yet another is examining the brand called Puffy jackets. Which product's demand is likely to be the least elastic? (a) jackets (b) Stay Warm jackets (c) Puffy jackets (d) It cannot be determined from the information given.   20._____

Part 3—Short Answer

Directions: Read the following questions and write several sentences in response.

21. How can increased gas prices have a greater income effect on high school students than on working professionals?

22. At what price per gallon would the typical high school student choose a substitute good for gasoline (ride a bike or use public transportation)? At what price per gallon would the working professional choose a substitute good for gasoline? Explain.

Part 4—Graphing

23. **Directions:** Consider the elasticity of demand for gasoline in the summertime as families plan summer vacations. (Demand is almost always more elastic at higher prices and less elastic at lower prices). Create a labeled graph depicting possible market demand for gasoline at various prices per gallon. ($1, $2, $3, and $4) Indicate the portion of the demand curve that illustrates elastic demand and the portion that illustrates inelastic demand.

Lesson 4.3 Changes in Demand

Part 1—True or False

Directions: Place a *T* for True or an *F* for False in the Answers column to show whether each of the following statements is true or false.

Answers

1. Consumer expectations rarely shift the demand curve.   1._____

2. The demand for an inferior good decreases as money income increases.   2._____

3. A large increase in births in one particular town would shift the demand curve for baby   3._____
   formula leftward.

4. The opportunity cost of a consumer's time must be explored when studying demand.   4._____

5. Pencils are the substitute goods for erasers.   5._____

6. If a population grows, the demand for food will shift leftward.   6._____

7. If a book borrowed from the library is a superior good, the same new book at a bookstore is   7._____
   an inferior good.

8. A rightward shift of the demand curve indicates that there is an increase in demand.   8._____

9. Products used in place of each other are referred to as complements.   9._____

10. A change in consumer income causes a movement along the demand curve.   10._____

Part 2—Multiple Choice

Directions: In the Answers column, write the letter that represents the word, or group of words, that correctly completes the statement or answers the question.

Answers

11. Which of the following determinants have the greatest effect on demand? (a) consumer tastes   11._____
    (b) number of consumers (c) consumer income (d) it cannot be determined from the
    information given

12. Which of the following pairs illustrates a normal good and a related inferior good, in that   12._____
    order? (a) used clothing and new, designer clothing (b) renting an apartment and taking a
    vacation (c) transportation using your own automobile and transportation using the subway
    (d) hiring an intern and hiring a professional

13. Suppose the media reports that in a matter of months, downloading music from the Internet   13._____
    will be completely legal and free. How might this announcement affect the demand curve for
    music CDs? (a) It would shift leftward. (b) It would shift downward. (c) It would shift
    rightward. (d) It would not be affected.

14. Which of the following goods are complements? (a) bananas and raisins (b) toothbrushes and   14._____
    toothpaste (c) watches and artwork (d) glasses and contact lenses

15. If the price of a particular good changes, which of the following will result? (a) movement   15._____
    along the demand curve (b) a shift of the demand curve (c) the demand curve becomes a
    vertical line (d) none of the previous

16. Which of the following would most likely cost the most? (a) buying vegetables at the grocery   16._____
    store to make stir-fry (b) buying a frozen stir-fry dinner and warming it up in the microwave
    (c) ordering a stir-fry dish from a restaurant (d) It cannot be determined from the information
    given.

17. Suppose that the media reports that JFK High School in Dallas is the number one high school   17._____
in the nation. How might this announcement affect the demand curve for houses in Dallas?
(a) It would shift to the left. (b) It would shift to the right. (c) It would not be affected. (d)
none of the previous

18. When people desire more of a product regardless of price there will be (a) a shift in the   18._____
product's demand curve to the right (b) movement up the product's demand curve (c) a shift
in the product's demand curve to the left (d) movement down the product's demand curve

19. Suppose there is an increase in the price of disposable diapers. How might the demand curve   19._____
for cloth diapers be affected? (a) It would shift leftward. (b) It would shift rightward. (c) It
would shift upward. (d) It would not be affected.

20. Suppose that after years of study, it is concluded that a low-carbohydrate diet reduces   20._____
cholesterol and contributes to overall health. How might the public's knowledge of such a
study affect the demand curve for white bread? (a) It would shift to the left. (b) It would shift
to the right. (c) It would shift up. (d) It would shift down.

Part 3—Short Answer

Directions: Read the following questions and write several sentences in response.

21. Provide an example of a normal good and an inferior good. How does an increase in income affect the
demand for each of these goods or services?

22. Provide two examples of the differences in the opportunity cost of time among consumers and how this
shapes different consumption patterns.

Part 4—Critical Thinking

23. **Directions:** A new rock-band, YoYo, just produced its second CD. Sketch two graphs to indicate the affect
that each determinant of demand will have on the demand curve. Write a sentence to describe the change in
demand. Determinants: (1) Prices of related goods (2) Consumer expectations

Name _____ Class _____ Date _____

Chapter Review

Part 1—True or False

Directions: Place a *T* for True or an *F* for False in the Answers column to show whether each of the following statements is true or false.

Answers

1. A jacket bought at a second-hand store is an inferior good.   1._____

2. If elasticity of demand is less than 1.0, then it can be described as unit-elastic.   2._____

3. According to the law of demand, quantity demanded varies inversely with price, all other   3._____
   things constant.

4. The demand for a normal good decreases as income increases.   4._____

5. Newspapers are substitute goods for magazines.   5._____

6. In order to calculate elasticity, one must be aware of how price is measured.   6._____

7. Diminishing marginal utility is defined as the satisfaction you derive from an additional unit of   7._____
   a product.

8. If the demand for cotton decreases during a certain time period, then the price of cotton will 8._____
   increase.

9. Demand is almost always less elastic at higher prices and more elastic at lower prices.   9._____

10. A change in one of the determinants of demand other than price causes a shift of the demand   10._____
    curve.

Part 2—Multiple Choice

Directions: In the Answers column, write the letter that represents the word, or group of words, that correctly completes the statement or answers the question.

Answers

11. Which scenario reflects the law of diminishing marginal utility? (a) You eat a hot dog and then   11._____
    order fries because you're still hungry. (b) You buy two boxes of cereal for the price of one.
    (c) Your mom offers you another baked potato at dinner, but you decline because you are full.
    (d) You buy a dozen donuts instead of eight donuts because it's cheaper that way.

12. Which of the following goods is the least price elastic? (a) cars (b) DVDs (c) cruise vacations   12._____
    (d) houses

13. Which of the following pairs illustrates a normal good and a related inferior good, in that   13._____
    order? (a) a laptop computer and a desktop computer (b) an automobile and a subway (c) a used
    paperback book and a new hardcover book (d) a sports utility vehicle and a truck

14. Angela is studying the market for sedans, Bonnie is researching the market for sports utility   14._____
    vehicles, and Carrie is studying the market for Ford trucks. Which product's demand is likely
    to be the most elastic? (a) sedans (b) sports utility vehicles (c) Ford trucks (d) It cannot be
    determined from the information given.

15. If a 7 percent change in the price of a product results in a 9 percent change in the quantity   15._____
    of the product that is demanded, then demand for the product is (a) inelastic (b) unit elastic
    (c) elastic (d) insensitive.

16. Which of the following goods are complements? (a) cameras and film (b) 7 Up and Coke   16._____
    (c) DVDs and videos (d) video games and gasoline

17. Which of the following would most likely cost the least? (a) going to an automatic car wash   17._____
    (b) going to a carwash whose employees wash your car by hand (c) going to a carwash where
    you wash your own car (d) washing your car at home in the driveway

18. When people's incomes increase there will be (a) movement up their demand curves for normal   18._____
    products (b) a shift to the right for their demand curves for normal products (c) movement
    down their demand curves for normal products (d) a shift to the left for their demand curves for
    normal products.

19. If the price of cat food increases from $.50 a can to $1 a can and the quantity demanded   19._____
    decreases from 4 million to 3 million, what is the elasticity of demand? (a) 4 (b) 1 (c) 0.75
    (d) 0.25

20. If your rent per month increases, which of the following is affected? (a) your marginal utility   20._____
    (b) your real income (c) your overall income (d) your money income

Part 3—Short Answer

Directions: Read the following questions and write several sentences in response.

21. Choose two products you use often. Identify a substitute and a related inferior good for each product.

22. Describe a situation you have encountered that illustrated the law of diminishing marginal utility.

Part 4—Critical Thinking

Directions: Leslie has started her own business selling hand-knit hats, scarves, and mittens. She begins
advertising in the local newspaper and, as a result, the demand for her products increases.

23. How is the demand curve affected?

Suppose that Leslie then lowers the price of her scarves from $15 to $10 per scarf. Her sales grow from 25
scarves per week to 50.

24. Calculate the elasticity of demand.

25. Determine if demand is elastic, unit elastic, or inelastic.

Lesson 5.1 The Supply Curve

Part 1—True or False

Directions: Place a *T* for True or an *F* for False in the Answers column to show whether each of the following statements is true or false.

Answers

1. If supply elasticity exceeds 1.0, then supply is unit elastic. 1._____

2. The law of supply states that as price increases, the amount supplied increases as well. 2._____

3. High prices discourage consumption but encourage production. 3._____

4. The terms "quantity supplied" and "quantity" are interchangeable. 4._____

5. The market supply curve shows the total quantity supplied by all producers at various prices. 5._____

6. Elasticity of supply is best defined as a measure of the responsiveness of quantity supplied to a price change. 6._____

7. The ease of increasing quantity supplied in response to a higher price differs across industries. 7._____

8. Economists assume that producers aim to maximize utility. 8._____

9. In order to calculate profit, a specific time period must be taken into consideration before any calculations are performed. 9._____

10. The marginal cost of production always decreases as output increases. 10._____

Part 2—Multiple Choice

Directions: In the Answers column, write the letter that represents the word, or group of words, that correctly completes the statement or answers the question.

Answers

11. A firm earns $8,000 in total revenue during a given week while spending a total cost of $7,600. Which of the following choices best describes how the firm is doing? (a) The firm is losing money overall. (b) The firm is breaking even. (c) The firm is earning a profit of 400. (d) The firm will soon go bankrupt. 11._____

12. Which of the following statements is true? (a) when price rises, producers cut back on their supply (b) profit is calculated by added total revenue to total cost (c) the elasticity of supply is always elastic (d) a normal supply curve slopes upward 12._____

13. Suppose that the price of a sweater at Sweater World decreases from $39.95 to $29.95. The quantity supplied decreases from 5 million to 2 million. Which of the following is the elasticity of supply? (a) 0.42 (b) 1.0 (c) 1.8 (d) 2.4 13._____

14. Using the information from item 13, which of the following choices best describes the elasticity of supply? (a) elastic (b) unit elastic (c) inelastic (d) it cannot be determined from the information given 14._____

15. How does an increase in price affect a producer? (a) The producer becomes more willing but less able to supply goods. (b) The producer becomes less willing but more able to supply goods. (c) The producer becomes more willing and more able to supply goods. (d) The producer becomes less willing and less able to supply goods. 15._____

16. A firm must achieve which of the following to remain open? (a) marginal cost must exceed marginal revenue (b) the firm avoids paying any fixed cost (c) total revenue should at least cover variable cost (d) none of the previous   16. _____

17. Suppose you are interested in researching how the increasing price of DVDs is affecting the DVD supply. Which of the following would you examine? (a) the market supply curve (b) the individual supply curve (c) the general supply curve (d) none of the previous   17. _____

18. Suppose that the price of bananas increases from $.25 per pound to $.75 per pound. The quantity supplied increases from 7 million to 10 million. Which of the following best describes the elasticity of supply? (a) unit elastic (b) inelastic (c) elastic (d) it cannot be determined from the information given   18. _____

Part 3—Short Answer

Directions: Read the following questions, and write your response.

19. What is the profit formula? How does the profit motive work as an incentive for producers to employ resources?

20. Explain how the rising price of in-ground swimming pools can act as a signal to potential suppliers?

21. Explain how the higher price of in-ground swimming pools increases the ability of potential suppliers to supply the good.

Part 5—Graphing

22. **Directions:** Graph the supply curve for J perfume by I Corporation. Describe the relationship between price and quantity supplied.

Price	200	175	150	100
Quantity supplied	2200	1500	1000	600

Lesson 5.2 Shifts of the Supply Curve

Part 1—True or False

Directions: Place a *T* for True or an *F* for False in the Answers column to show whether each of the following statements is true or false.

Answers

1. A rightward shift of the supply curve indicates a decrease in supply.   1. _____

2. An increase in supply means that producers are more willing and able to supply a good at each   2. _____
    price.

3. The cost of resources used to make a good is the only determinant that affects market supply.   3. _____

4. A decrease in the price of DVD players would shift the VCR supply curve rightward.   4. _____

5. Improvements in technology cause an upward movement along a given supply curve.   5. _____

6. If automobile producers expected car prices to increase in the future, economists would expect   6. _____
    to see a shift of the supply curve.

7. An increase in business taxes would mean fewer lawyers opening their own firms.   7. _____

8. The use of credit-card technology at fast-food restaurants will likely cause a movement along   8. _____
    the supply curve.

9. A change in a determinant of supply other than price causes a movement along a supply curve.   9. _____

10. Government restrictions that limit the number of companies that can produce airplanes are   10._____
    relaxed. Therefore, the supply of airplanes increases.

Part 2—Multiple Choice

Directions: In the Answers column, write the letter that represents the word, or group of words, that correctly completes the statement or answers the question.

Answers

11. If cabbage farmers expect the price cabbage to decrease in the near future, which of the   11._____
    following actions would the producers most likely take? (a) they would probably do nothing
    (b) they would store the majority of the cabbage produced (c) they would decrease production
    capacity immediately (d) they would increase production capacity immediately

12. Suppose the price of a certain good decreases. Which of the following would result? (a)   12._____
    movement along the supply curve (b) the supply curve would change shape (c) a shift of the
    supply curve (d) none of the previous

13. If a company that produces jelly sees the price of strawberries decreases, what would happen   13._____
    to the company's supply of apricot jelly? (a) it would decrease (b) it would increase (c) it
    would remain constant (d) it cannot be determined from the information given

14. If the government imposed strict rules on how many farmers may produce blueberries, what   14._____
    would happen to the supply of blueberries? (a) It would increase. (b) It would decrease. (c) It
    would remain constant. (d) It would decrease immediately and then increase.

15. Research during a ten-year period concludes that Drug X, used for treating depression, is harmful. The company that produces Drug X also produces Drug Y, which also treats depression. What would happen to the supply curve for Drug Y? (a) it would shift leftward (b) it would shift rightward (c) there would be a movement along the curve (d) it would not be affected   15._____

16. If there was an increase in the price of lumber, how would this affect the supply curve of houses? (a) it would shift rightward (b) it would shift leftward (c) it would not be affected (d) it cannot be determined from the information given   16._____

17. Which of the following does **not** cause a shift of the supply curve? (a) a change in the cost of resources needed to produce the good (b) a change in the expectations of producers (c) a change in technology used to make a good (d) a change in price of the good   17._____

18. A new machine that decreases the time it takes to produce a specific airplane engine part is introduced into the market. What would most likely happen to the supply of this part? (a) it would increase (b) it would decrease (c) it would remain constant (d) it cannot be determined from the information given   18._____

19. What effect might the Clean Diamond Trade Act that requires additional testing for the purity of diamonds have on the supply of diamonds in the United States? (a) little or no effect (b) supply would increase (c) supply would decrease (d) none of the previous   19._____

20. The price of compact cars increases. What would most likely happen to the supply curve for Sports Utility Vehicles)? (a) shift rightward (b) shift leftward (c) no effect (d) It cannot be determined from the information given.   20._____

Part 3—Short Answer

Directions: Read the following questions, and write your response.

21. List some alternative uses for leather that a producer might consider as relative prices vary.

22. What is the difference between a change in supply and a change in quantity supplied?

Part 5—Graphing

Directions: Name the determinant of supply described in the following scenarios. Create a supply curve and a shift in supply if applicable. (New supply curves should be labeled S_1.)

23. The price of the perfume ingredient ylang-ylang increases.	24. Four new perfumes are introduced to the market this fall season.

_____

Lesson ● 5.3 Production and Cost

_____

Part 1—True or False

Directions: Place a *T* for True or an *F* for False in the Answers column to show whether each of the following statements is true or false.

Answers

1. In the long run, no resources are fixed.   1._____

2. Marginal product is always positive.   2._____

3. Total product increases with every additional worker hired, without exception.   3._____

4. A competitive firm's marginal revenue is usually the market price of a product.   4._____

5. The marginal cost of production always falls as output increases.   5._____

6. Firms normally produce in the range of diminishing but positive marginal returns.   6._____

7. A fixed cost usually changes in the short run.   7._____

8. Firms try to avoid diseconomies of scale.   8._____

9. Firms plan for the short run, but they produce in the long run.   9._____

10. The law of diminishing returns states that as more units of one resource are added to all other 10._____
    resources, marginal product eventually increases.

_____

Part 2—Multiple Choice

Directions: In the Answers column, write the letter that represents the word, or group of words, that correctly completes the statement or answers the question.

Answers

11. What is the total cost if the fixed cost of a firm is $700 and the variable cost is $450? (a)   11._____
    $250 (b) $175 (c) $1,150 (d) $700

12. ___?___ is an example of a variable resource. (a) number of offices (b) number of machines   12._____
    in a factory (c) the size of a factory (d) number of workers

13. ____?___ most accurately defines fixed cost. (a) a production cost that is independent of the   13._____
    firm's output (b) a production cost that changes as output changes (c) the change in total cost
    that results from a one-unit change in output (d) the change in total revenue from selling
    another unit of a good

14. Suppose increasing output from 200 to 300 units increases total cost by $300. What is the   14._____
    marginal cost? (a) $.33 (b) $3 (c) $66 (d) $1

15. Which of the following defines economies of scale? (a) the change in total revenue from   15._____
    selling an additional unit of a good (b) the upward sloping portion of a firm's marginal cost
    curve at and above the minimum acceptable price (c) forces that reduce a firm's average cost
    as the firm's size increases in the long-run (d) the lowest average cost of producing each
    output when the firm's size is allowed to vary

16. If a firm's long-run average cost increases as production increases, which of the following is   16._____
    reflected? (a) economies of scale (b) marginal revenue (c) diseconomies of scale (d)
    marginal cost

17. Producers will sell additional units as long as which of the following is happening? (a) the marginal revenue they receive exceeds the marginal cost (b) the marginal cost they receive exceeds the marginal revenue (c) the marginal cost equals the marginal revenue (d) none of the previous

17._____

18. What happens to the fixed cost of a firm that is temporarily shut down? (a) fixed cost increases (b) fixed cost decreases (c) fixed cost remains constant (d) none of the previous

18._____

19. Which of the following is a function of a long-run average cost curve? (a) it reduces a firm's average cost as the firm's size increases in the long run (b) it allows the firm to cover variable costs (c) it is identical to a supply curve (d) it indicates the lowest average cost of production at each rate of output when a firm's size is allowed to vary

19._____

20. Which of the following is an example of a variable cost? (a) insurance (b) rent (c) labor (d) equipment

20._____

Part 3—Short Answer

Directions: Read the following questions, and write your response.

21. Why does total output for a firm lessen as more and more workers are added to the production process?

22. What do changes in marginal cost reflect?

23. Explain the statement, "the firm settles on the level of output where marginal revenue equals marginal cost."

24. Why are there no fixed costs in the long run?

Part 4—Graphing

25. **Directions:** Create a long-run average cost curve and label the three parts as follows: (A) economies of scale, (B) minimum efficient scale, (C) diseconomies of scale.

Name _____ Class _____ Date_____

_____

Chapter ⑤ Review

_____

Part 1—True or False

Directions: Place a *T* for True or an *F* for False in the Answers column to show whether each of the following statements is true or false.

Answers

1. The introduction of an electronic diagnostic system in a car repair shop will most likely cause a movement along the supply curve.

   1._____

2. Total product can decrease with the addition of one or more workers.

   2._____

3. According to the law of supply, if the price of bananas increases, the amount supplied decreases.

   3._____

4. A decrease in the cost of producing a product will cause the supply curve for that product to shift to the right.

   4._____

5. For a firm to continue to produce, total revenue should at least cover variable cost.

   5._____

6. The cost of resources needed to make a good does not affect market supply.

   6._____

7. A clerk's wage is an example of a fixed cost in the short run.

   7._____

8. The elasticity of supply usually decreases over a long period of adjustment.

   8._____

9. A change in the expectations of producers causes a movement along the supply curve.

   9._____

10. Economies of scale are forces that reduce a firm's average cost as the firm's size increases in the long run.

    10._____

_____

Part 2—Multiple Choice

Directions: In the Answers column, write the letter that represents the word, or group of words, that correctly completes the statement or answers the question.

Answers

11. Which of the following would cause the market supply curve for eggs to shift to the left? (a) A new study determines that eggs do not have as much cholesterol as researchers once thought. (b) A new drug is introduced to increase the fertility of chickens. (c) Twenty percent of the nation's chickens die from an outbreak of disease (d) none of the previous.

    11._____

12. What is the total cost if the fixed cost of a firm is $2,700 and the variable cost is $1,000? (a) $3,700 (b) $2,700 (c) $1,000 (d) $1,700.

    12._____

13. The supply curve slopes upward because (a) as price increases, supply decreases (b) producers supply more of a product at a higher price than at a lower price (c) demand becomes more elastic over time (d) none of the previous.

    13._____

14. A company that produces comforters sees the price of down feathers increase. Therefore, the company's supply of down comforters would (a) increase (b) decrease (c) stay constant (d) It cannot be determined from the information given.

    14._____

15. Which of the following is an example of a variable cost? (a) mortgage payments (b) computers (c) labor (d) insurance

    15._____

16. If the price of ground beef increases, how would the supply curve for ground beef be affected? (a) It would shift leftward. (b) It would shift rightward. (c) There would be movement along the curve. (d) It would not be affected.   16._____

17. Suppose that tomato growers expect the price of tomatoes to increase in the near future. What action might they take? (a) immediately increase production capacity (b) immediately decrease production capacity (c) store the majority of tomatoes they produce (d) probably do nothing.   17._____

18. If a firm currently supplies 500 products at $10, but supplies 1,000 products when it raises its price to $15, the elasticity of supply is (a) elastic (b) unit elastic (c) inelastic (d) equal to 1   18._____

19. The government repeals a law that has restricted the amount of wheat that can be grown in the United States. This would cause the supply of wheat to (a) increase (b) decrease (c) remain constant (d) It cannot be determined from the information given.   19._____

20. If increasing output from 300 to 400 units increases total cost by $150, then what is the marginal cost? (a) $1 (b) $150 (c) $.01 (d) $1.50   20._____

Part 3—Short Answer

Directions: Read the following questions, and write your response.

21. Identify a food product that your family often buys. What might cause your grocery store to increase its supply of this product?

22. Suppose you decide to open your own business. What would you have to achieve in order to keep that business afloat?

Part 4—Critical Thinking

23. Suppose you open a small shop that sells chocolates. Your monthly fixed costs total $2,500. You pay one employee $1,000 per month and your total revenue from sales last month was $3,000. Should you continue to operate your business or shut it down? Explain.

Lesson ⬤6.1 Price, Quantity, and Market Equilibrium

Part 1—True or False

Directions: Place a *T* for True or an *F* for False in the Answers column to show whether each of the following statements is true or false.

Answers

1. The demand and supply curves intersect at the equilibrium point.   1._____

2. Consumer surplus is defined as the difference between the total amount consumers would be willing and able to pay for that quantity and the total amount they actually do pay.   2._____

3. A market finds equilibrium through the independent and voluntary actions of a small amount of buyers and sellers.   3._____

4. Markets distribute earnings among resource owners.   4._____

5. An equilibrium price is achieved when quantity supplied is equal to quantity demanded.   5._____

6. Prices help both producers and consumers recognize what's happening in the market and make choices based on this information.   6._____

7. A surplus takes any pressure off the market that might cause the price of a good to change.   7._____

8. A shortage results when the quantity demanded exceeds the quantity supplied.   8._____

9. Only consumers benefit from the market, not producers.   9._____

10. Once an equilibrium price is reached, it will no longer change in the future.   10._____

Part 2—Multiple Choice

Directions: In the Answers column, write the letter that represents the word, or group of words, that correctly completes the statement or answers the question.

Answers

11. What will happen to the price of a good when there is a shortage of that good? (a) The price decreases. (b) The price increases. (c) The price will not be affected. (d) It cannot be determined from the information given.   11._____

12. If a company that produces high-end pajamas supplies 5 million pairs but consumers demand 2 million pairs of pajamas, which of the following describes the result of this situation? (a) shortage of pajamas (b) surplus of pajamas (c) the market has reached equilibrium (d) none of the previous   12._____

13. Which of the following parties drives markets? (a) buyers (b) producers (c) sellers (d) all of the previous   13._____

14. A firm that produces lightweight glasses frames supplies 10 million frames. However, consumers demand 11 million frames. Which of the following statements describes the result of this situation? (a) shortage of frames (b) surplus of frames (c) the market has reached equilibrium (d) none of the previous   14._____

Part 3—Short Answer

Directions: Place an arrow ↑ or an arrow ↓ in the spaces below. Indicate whether a shortage or surplus would result by underlining the correct word.

15. The equilibrium price for cheesecake is $8.50 and the equilibrium quantity is 1000. At $6.50, there would be a (shortage/surplus) placing _____ pressure on price. At $9.00 there would be a (shortage/surplus) placing _____ pressure on price.

16. Why is equilibrium price also referred to as the market-clearing price?

Part 4—Critical Thinking

Directions: Read the following questions, and write your response.

17. Provide an example that illustrates the statement, "Buyers and sellers direct resources and products to those who value them most."

18. Describe some of the transaction costs involved in purchasing a new car.

Part 5—Graphing

19. **Directions:** Create a graph for holiday jewelry sets from the schedule below. Then answer the questions.

Price	Quantity demanded	Quantity supplied
$14	3000	50
$16	1500	500
$18	1000	1000
$20	500	1500
$22	100	3000

20. At $16 there is a shortage because quantity demanded is (a) less than (b) equal to (c) greater than _____ quantity supplied.

21. At $20, there is a surplus because quantity demanded is (a) less than (b) equal to (c) greater than _____ quantity supplied.

22. The market clearing price is $18 because quantity demanded is (a) less than quantity supplied (b) equal to quantity supplied (c) greater than quantity supplied. _____

Lesson (6.2) Shifts of Demand and Supply Curves

Part 1—True or False

Directions: Place a *T* for True or an *F* for False in the Answers column to show whether each of the following statements is true or false.

Answers

1. If both the demand and supply curves of chocolate shift to the left, the equilibrium quantity will decrease.   1._____

2. Technological breakthroughs can shift a demand curve but not a supply curve.   2._____

3. A decrease in the price of ketchup could affect the demand for French fries.   3._____

4. An increase in the number of shops that sell coats in one mall could shift the supply curve for coats.   4._____

5. The leftward shift of a given supply curve reduces price and increases quantity.   5._____

6. Changes in technology usually have no effect on any given supply curve.   6._____

7. If both demand and supply increase, the equilibrium quantity will always increase.   7._____

8. If the demand and supply curves shift in opposite directions, equilibrium quantity will always increase.   8._____

9. If both the demand and supply curves shift to the left, but the demand curve shifts more than the supply curve, the equilibrium price will decrease.   9._____

10. If both the supply and demand curves shift rightward, but the supply curve shifts more than the demand curve, equilibrium price will decrease.   10._____

Part 2—Multiple Choice

Directions: In the Answers column, write the letter that represents the word, or group of words, that correctly completes the statement or answers the question.

Answers

11. Both the demand curve and the supply curve for pencils shift rightward. How is the price of pencils affected? (a) price increases (b) price decreases (c) price stays constant (d) It cannot be determined from the information given.   11._____

12. Which of the following situations could shift the demand curve for dental floss? (a) an increase in the number of people who use dental floss (b) the release of a study that says flossing significantly reduces the risk of gum disease (c) an increase in the price of mouthwash (d) all of the previous   12._____

13. While the demand curve for a sports magazine shifts rightward, the supply curve also moves rightward but to a greater degree. This would cause equilibrium price to (a) decrease (b) increase (c) stay constant (d) It cannot be determined from the information given.   13._____

14. An automobile plant employs most of the people in a town. The plant suddenly shuts down production. What effects might a local burger joint feel as a result? (a) The demand for burgers would increase. (b) The demand curve for burgers would shift leftward. (c) The demand curve would shift rightward. (d) The demand curve would not be affected.   14._____

15. Suppose the supply and demand curves for cameras shift leftward. As a result, equilibrium quantity (a) increases (b) stays constant (c) decreases (d) cannot be determined   15._____

16. If the price of vitamins decreases while the quantity demanded increases, how would this be 16. _____
    reflected in the supply curve? (a) The supply curve would shift leftward. (b) The supply curve
    would shift rightward. (c) The supply curve would not be affected. (d) none of the previous

Part 3—Short Answer

Directions: Label each of the following statements with a D if it describes a determinant of demand or an S if it describes a determinant of supply. Use an arrow up ↑ or an arrow down ↓ to indicate shifts in demand or supply.

Answers

17. Income tax refunds lead to increased purchases of personal computers. 17. _____

18. The names of many new children fill waiting lists for childcare facilities. 18. _____

19. A new packaging machine increases production of candy canes. 19. _____

20. A news article about filthy conditions in a local restaurants alarms customers. 20. _____

21. An increase in the price of oranges has a negative effect on orange juice production. 21. _____

Part 4—Graphing

22. **Directions:** Produce a demand and supply curve for each statement at the right. Do not use values for prices or quantities, and indicate the equilibrium point for each graph. Use a dashed line to illustrate an increase in demand. Use a dotted line to indicate a decrease in supply. Indicate the new equilibrium point. What affect do the new curves have on the price and quantity?

Demand increases more than supply, price increases, quantity increases.

Supply decreases more than demand, price increases, quantity decreases.

Supply and demand increase in same increments, price increases, quantity stays the same.

Lesson 6.3 Market Efficiency and Gains from Exchange

Part 1—True or False

Directions: Place a *T* for True or an *F* for False in the Answers column to show whether each of the following statements is true or false.

Answers

1. Market exchange usually benefits both consumers and producers.   1._____

2. If the government was concerned about affordable housing, it might enact a price floor.   2._____

3. It has been shown that charging people on Medicaid a small amount of money for visits to the doctor has no effect on their number of visits.   3._____

4. A price floor must be set below the equilibrium price to be effective.   4._____

5. Disequilibrium is a permanent condition.   5._____

6. Producing at the lowest possible cost per unit is no guarantee that firms are producing what consumers most prefer.   6._____

7. Achieving productive efficiency guarantees success in the market.   7._____

8. Most of the time, when something is provided for free, people consume it until their marginal benefit is zero.   8._____

9. When a firm achieves allocative efficiency, it is "making the right stuff."   9._____

10. Government intervention always puts an end to shortages and surpluses.   10._____

Part 2—Multiple Choice

Directions: In the Answers column, write the letter that represents the word, or group of words, that correctly completes the statement or answers the question.

Answers

11. A price ceiling set below the equilibrium price causes which of the following? (a) a surplus (b) a shortage (c) equilibrium (d) none of the previous   11._____

12. An art gallery offers the most modern art at the lowest prices per unit in the city, but sales are low. At the same time the gallery's demand for Victorian art has increased. With which of the following concepts is the company most likely struggling? (a) consumer surplus (b) marginal cost (c) allocative efficiency (d) productive efficiency   12._____

13. If the opportunities for employment among independent building contractors are extremely low, what could the government do to help these contractors achieve a stable income? (a) undertake new public building projects (b) enact a consumer surplus (c) encourage productive efficiency (d) enact a price ceiling   13._____

14. Which of the following terms refers to producing output at the lowest possible cost? (a) productive efficiency (b) consumer surplus (c) allocative efficiency (d) price ceiling   14._____

15. Which of the following could cause disequilibrium? (a) actions taken by the government (b) the introduction of a new product into the market (c) a sudden and sharp rise in demand (d) all of the previous   15._____

16. Which of the following guarantees allocative efficiency? (a) productive efficiency (b) market competition (c) marginal cost (d) none of the previous   16._____

Part 3—Fill in the Blank

Directions: In the space provided, write the word or phrase that best completes each statement.

17. Productive efficiency refers to firms that produce at the lowest _____.

18. Allocative efficiency refers to producing output that consumers most _____.

19. _____ refers to the benefit consumers enjoy when they get to purchase goods at prices below what they are willing and able to pay.

Part 5—Critical Thinking

Directions: Read the following questions, and write your response.

20. Why is a price "floor" above the equilibrium point, and a price "ceiling" below the equilibrium point?

21. Why do price ceilings lead to shortages? What is an example of a price ceiling?

22. Why do price floors lead to surpluses? What is an example of a price floor?

Part 5—Graphing

Directions: Examine the schedule for a popular product known as "Gibs."

Price	Quantity demanded	Quantity supplied
$ .50	50	20
$ .75	45	25
$1.00	35	30
$1.25	35	35
$1.50	30	40
$1.75	25	45

23. What would be the effect of a price ceiling at $1.75?

24. What would be the effect of a price floor at $.75?

Chapter 6 Review

Part 1—True or False

Directions: Place a *T* for True or an *F* for False in the Answers column to show whether each of the following statements is true or false.

Answers

1. Technological breakthroughs can shift both a supply and demand curve.   1._____
2. The market is allocatively efficient when the marginal benefit that consumers derive from a good equals the marginal cost of producing that good.   2._____
3. A surplus results when the quantity demanded exceeds the quantity supplied.   3._____
4. A decrease in the demand for computers will cause the supply curve for computers to shift.   4._____
5. A change in producers' expectations will cause the supply curve to shift but not the demand curve.   5._____
6. A price ceiling set below the equilibrium price will cause a shortage.   6._____
7. Markets increase transaction costs.   7._____
8. Prices help consumers, but not sellers, to recognize market opportunities.   8._____
9. Buyers, producers, and sellers drive markets.   9._____
10. Allocative efficiency means producing output at the lowest possible cost.   10._____

Part 2—Multiple Choice

Directions: In the Answers column, write the letter that represents the word, or group of words, that correctly completes the statement or answers the question.

Answers

11. Which scenario would cause the market for fish tanks to clear? (a) 150 fish tanks are demanded and 150 fish tanks are supplied (b) 150 fish tanks are demanded and 100 fish tanks are supplied (c) 150 fish tanks are demanded and 200 fish tanks are supplied (d) 150 fish tanks are demanded and 300 fish tanks are supplied.   11._____

12. If both the demand curve and the supply curve for cameras shift rightward, how is the price of cameras affected? (a) price increases (b) price decreases (c) price remains the same (d) It cannot be determined from the information given.   12._____

13. Suppose a new type of CD player that has just come onto the market is in high demand during the holiday season. Although it originally sold for $199.99, stores have hiked prices dramatically. What action could the government take to prevent this? (a) establish a price floor (b) establish a disequilibrium (c) establish a price ceiling (d) establish consumer surplus   13._____

14. If the cost of producing baseball cards declines (a) the supply curve for baseball cards will shift to the right and their price will fall (b) the supply curve for baseball cards will shift to the left and their price will fall (c) the supply curve for baseball cards will shift to the right and their price will increase (d) the supply curve for baseball cards will shift to the left and their price will increase   14._____

15. A firm produces 8,000 jars of baby food, but consumers demand 6,000. What will most likely result? (a) an equilibrium (b) a surplus (c) a shortage (d) none of the previous   15._____

16. Using the information from item 15, what will most likely happen to the price of a jar of baby   16.____
    food? (a) increase (b) decrease (c) remain constant (d) none of the previous

17. A decrease in the price of tacos might affect the supply curve for (a) chocolate cake (b) books   17.____
    (c) pizza (d) coal

18. If the equilibrium price for a gallon of paint is $20 and the equilibrium quantity is 7 million,   18.____
    what is the market-clearing price for a gallon of paint? (a) $7 (b) $15 (c) $27 (d) $20

19. If the demand curve for swimsuits shifts rightward and the supply curve also moves   19.____
    rightward but to a greater degree, how is the equilibrium price affected? (a) it will decrease
    (b) it will increase (c) it will stay the same (d) it cannot be determined from the information
    given

20. If there is a surplus for a good, what will happen to the price of that good? (a) decrease   20.____
    (b) increase (c) stay the same (d) It cannot be determined from the information given.

Part 3—Short Answer

Directions: Read the following scenario, and write your response.

21. Describe how markets affect transaction costs.

22. Identify two scenarios that would shift the airline ticket supply curve.

Part 4—Critical Thinking

23. Complete the chart below.

Price per pair of socks	Quantity demanded	Quantity supplied	Surplus or shortage?	Will price rise or fall?
$5.00	500	700		
$4.50	570	650		
$4.00	610	610		
$3.50	660	500		
$3.00	700	400		

Lesson 7.1   Perfect Competition and Monopoly

Part 1—True or False

Directions: Place a *T* for True or an *F* for False in the Answers column to show whether each of the following statements is true or false.

                                                                  Answers

1. A perfect competitor has no market power.   1._____

2. Monopolies can be beneficial.   2._____

3. A natural monopoly may emerge from the nature of costs.   3._____

4. The government can never make it illegal to enter a particular market.   4._____

5. The government itself may be a monopolist.   5._____

6. Monopolies never go bankrupt.   6._____

7. A television is an example of a commodity.   7._____

8. There are more perfect monopolies in the United States than competitive firms.   8._____

9. In perfect competition there are many buyers and sellers.   9._____

10. The demand curve for monopolists' output also is the market demand curve.   10._____

Part 2—Multiple Choice

Directions: In the Answers column, write the letter that represents the word, or group of words, that correctly completes the statement or answers the question.

                                                                  Answers

11. Which of the following is true? (a) There are high barriers to entry in a monopolized market. (b) Monopolies have little market power. (c) The monopoly market structure and the perfect competition structure are identical. (d) Governments never confer monopoly rights to markets.   11._____

12. How do the prices for goods produced by monopolies typically compare to the prices for goods produced by perfectly competitive firm? (a) Monopolies' goods are usually more expensive. (b) Monopolies' goods are usually less expensive. (c) Monopolies' goods are usually priced the same as perfectly competitive firms' goods. (d) none of the previous   12._____

13. Which of the following is true about a perfectly competitive market? (a) Firms produce standardized commodities. (b) Not all sellers are fully informed about technology. (c) One individual buyer or seller can usually influence price. (d) It is difficult for firms to enter the market.   13._____

14. What does the demand curve for an individual corn farmer look like? (a) vertical line (b) upward sloping line (c) horizontal line (d) downward sloping line   14._____

15. Which of the following may result from the success of a monopoly? (a) resources are wasted (b) lack of innovation (c) inefficiency (d) all of the previous   15._____

16. Which of the following markets is **not** likely to be an example of perfect competition? (a) foreign exchange (b) agricultural products (c) a large corporation (d) All of the previous are examples of perfect competition.   16._____

17. Which of these is an example of a geographic monopoly? (a) the market for wheat (b) the sole grocery store in a town (c) Western Electric Co. (d) the market for British currency   17._____

18. Why might a monopolist keep price below the profit-maximizing level? (a) to encourage government regulation (b) to expand the number of firms in the market (c) to avoid attracting   18._____

competitors (d) none of the previous

19. Which of the following best describes the U.S. Postal Service? (a) a perfectly competitive firm 19._____
(b) monopoly (c) holding little market power (d) all of the previous

Part 3—Short Answer

Directions: Read the following questions, and write your response.

20. What are the four features that identify different market structures?

21. What keeps competitors from entering a monopoly-controlled market?

Part 4—Critical Thinking

Directions: Read the following questions, and write your response.

22.. Why is first-class mail delivery by the U.S. Postal Service considered to be a monopoly market structure?

23. Why do natural monopolies sometimes emerge and how does market demand affect these firms?

Part 5—Graphing

24. **Directions:** Create a graph that would illustrate the demand curve for one producer of soybeans at a perfectly competitive market price of $3 a bushel.

Lesson 7.2 Monopolistic Competition and Oligopoly

Part 1—True or False

Directions: Place a *T* for True or an *F* for False in the Answers column to show whether each of the following statements is true or false.

Answers

1. Cartels are illegal in the United States.   1._____

2. There are high barriers to entry in the market in perfect competition.   2._____

3. Firms in monopolistic competition can leave the market easily in the long run.   3._____

4. A differentiated oligopoly sells products that differ across producers.   4._____

5. An oligopoly is a market dominated by just a few firms.   5._____

6. Firms in monopolistic competition never operate with excess capacity.   6._____

7. The market for breakfast cereals is an example of undifferentiated oligopoly.   7._____

8. Firms in monopolistic competition must take the reaction of other firms into account when deciding on price.   8._____

9. A firm operating at minimum efficient scale is taking advantage of economies of scale.   9._____

10. OPEC is an example of a cartel.   10._____

Part 2—Multiple Choice

Directions: In the Answers column, write the letter that represents the word, or group of words, that correctly completes the statement or answers the question.

Answers

11. Which of the following markets is an example of an oligopoly? (a) electronics (b) tobacco (c) book publishers (d) farmers   11._____

12. How many firms are in a monopoly? (a) one (b) two (c) three (d) unlimited number   12._____

13. Which of the following helps oligopolistic firms to decrease competition and increase profit? (a) creating a surplus (b) decreasing barriers to entry (c) collusion (d) increasing product differentiation   13._____

14. Which of the following is true about monopolistic competition? (a) each firm's demand curve slopes upward (b) firms do not have control over price (c) barriers to entry into the market are low (d) all of the previous   14._____

15. Which of the following is an example of monopolistic competition? (a) phone service (b) corn (c) shares of stock (d) books   15._____

16. Which of the following has the most number of firms? (a) monopoly (b) monopolistic competition (c) perfect competition (d) oligopoly   16._____

17. If a company that makes skateboards wants its product to stand out from other brands of skateboards, which of the following might it do? (a) make their skateboards available at a variety of stores (b) create unusual packaging (c) boost the skateboard's image by getting a celebrity endorsement (d) all of the previous   17._____

18. What do economists believe causes an oligopolistic market structure? (a) economies of scale (b) barriers to entry (c) high cost of entering the market (d) all of the previous   18._____

19. Which of the following usually results from colluding firms? (a) more is produced (b) profit decreases (c) prices are higher (d) more firms enter the market   19._____

20. Which of the following is a valid criticism of monopolistic competition? (a) Although firms try to claim that their products differ significantly from others, they usually do not. (b) It boosts prices up to a very high level. (c) It decreases the consumer's range of choices. (d) It does not allow firms to use their resources efficiently.   20._____

Part 3—Short Answer

Directions: Read the following questions, and write your response.

21. How does the market structure of monopolistic competition contain elements of both "monopoly" and "competition"?

22. Why do firms in monopolistic competition typically operate with excess capacity?

23. What is the difference between an undifferentiated oligopoly and a differentiated oligopoly?

24. Why do oligopolists spend large amounts to advertise their products?

Part 4—Critical Thinking

Directions: Read the following questions, and write your response.

25. How can a firm introducing a new frozen pizza product to the market differentiate their product?

26. Explain the interdependence of three rival firms in an oligopoly market structure.

27. Why are cartels and collusion deemed illegal in the United States?

28. Why do you think efforts to form cartels in the world markets for copper and coffee have failed?

Lesson   7.3   Antitrust, Economic Regulation, and Competition

Part 1—True or False

Directions: Place a *T* for True or an *F* for False in the Answers column to show whether each of the following statements is true or false.

Answers

1. Technological improvements often cause firms to be more competitive.   1._____

2. Natural monopolies are not regulated.   2._____

3. Federal antitrust officials are able to approve or deny mergers.   3._____

4. Deregulation, for the most part, has decreased competition.   4._____

5. Antitrust laws can benefit both consumers and producers.   5._____

6. Banking is an industry that has experienced deregulation.   6._____

7. Two companies that produce completely different things can merge.   7._____

8. The U.S. Justice Department found Microsoft not guilty of violating antitrust laws.   8._____

9. The number of industries considered competitive has increased in the past 40 years.   9._____

10. Firms that control supplies of raw materials tend to be more competitive.   10._____

Part 2—Multiple Choice

Directions: In the Answers column, write the letter that represents the word, or group of words, that correctly completes the statement or answers the question.

Answers

11. Which of the following is an example of a horizontal merger? (a) AT&T and MCI (b) NBC and General Motors (c) CVS and Procter and Gamble (d) Little Publishing and Mobil gasoline   11._____

12. What has contributed to an increase in competition over the past few decades? (a) a decrease in regulation (b) a decrease in antitrust activity (c) a decrease in technological change (d) a decease in international trade   12._____

13. Technology in network television programming has improved over the past few decades. How has this affected network television stations? (a) size of audiences has increased. (b) size of audiences has decreased (c) size of audiences has not been affected(d) none of the previous   13._____

14. Which of the following resulted when Congress passed the Airline Deregulation Act? (a) fewer airline seats were filled (b) airlines became less productive (c) passenger miles decreased by half (d) prices of airfares decreased   14._____

15. The goal of antitrust activity is to (a) decrease competition in the marketplace (b) prevent exploitation of consumers by monopolies (c) create cartels (d) all of the previous.   15._____

16. What effect has international trade had on U.S. automobile companies? (a) U.S.-made cars are offered at more competitive prices. (b) Producers have improved the quality of U.S.-made cars. (c) Companies have found new ways to compete with foreign automobile companies. (a) all of the previous   16._____

17. ___?___ is defined as a combination of two or more firms to join as a single firm. (a) Antitrust (b) Deregulation (c) Merger (d) Special interest   17._____

18. ___?___ is **not** one of the early antitrust laws? (a) the Federal Trade Commission Act (b) the   18._____
Sherman Antitrust Act (c) the Clayton Act (d) the Douglas Antitrust Act

19. ___?___ is a goal of deregulation. (a) Enforcing stronger restrictions on firms that wish to   19._____
merge (b) Decreasing competition in the marketplace (c) Eliminating government regulations
(d) Lower gas prices

20. The Internet has affected competition between firms by (a) increasing competition   20._____
(b) decreasing competition (c) not affecting competition significantly (d) raising prices

Part 3—Short Answer

Directions: Read the following questions, and write your response.

21. What are the two goals of antitrust activity?

22. Differentiate between "horizontal mergers" and "nonhorizontal mergers."

23. What does the government hope to achieve in regulating natural monopolies?

Part 4—Critical Thinking

Directions: Read the following questions, and write your response.

24. Explain why this quote is true. "The U.S. economy has grown more competitive in the last half century."

25. Compare and contrast the view that government regulation is in the public interest with the view that it serves special interests of producers.

26. How could the deregulation of the U.S. Post Office lower prices and improve the product?

Name _____ Class _____ Date _____

Chapter Review

Part 1—True or False

Directions: Place a *T* for True or an *F* for False in the Answers column to show whether each of the following statements is true or false.

Answers

1. A market that is an oligopoly consists of many firms.   1._____

2. The Federal Trade Commission Act is one of the earliest antitrust laws.   2._____

3. Monopolies can never be beneficial to the economy.   3._____

4. Only companies that produce the same types of goods can merge.   4._____

5. Deregulation has increased competition within the marketplace.   5._____

6. In perfect competition there are many obstacles preventing new firms from entering profitable markets.   6._____

7. A lack of innovation may result from a successful monopoly.   7._____

8. Goods produced by a monopoly usually are more expensive than those produced by a perfectly competitive firm.   8._____

9. Antitrust laws aim to decrease competition in the marketplace.   9._____

10. A monopolist might keep price below the profit-maximizing level to avoid attracting competitors.   10._____

Part 2—Multiple Choice

Directions: In the Answers column, write the letter that represents the word, or group of words, that correctly completes the statement or answers the question.

Answers

11. Which of the following is an example of a geographic monopoly? (a) AT&T (b) Microsoft (c) the only bowling alley in a town (d) an Italian restaurant in Manhattan   11._____

12. How might a sneaker company make its product stand out from other brands of sneakers? (a) create unusual packaging (b) gain an endorsement from a famous athlete (c) merge with other companies (d) all of the previous   12._____

13. What does the demand curve for a dairy farmer look like? (a) upward sloping line (b) downward sloping line (c) vertical line (d) horizontal line   13._____

14. Which of the following is an example of a horizontal merger? (a) US Airways and CBS (b) McDonald's and Burger King (c) Home Depot and Macy's (d) NBC and GE   14._____

15. In a perfectly competitive market, (a) there are high barriers to entry (b) firms produce standardized commodities (c) individual buyers can influence price (d) all producers earn the same profits   15._____

16. An oligopolistic market structure is caused by (a) the low cost of market entry (b) a lack of competition in the marketplace (c) economies of scale (d) government regulation   16._____

17. A merger is defined as (a) a combination of two or more firms that join as a single firm (b) a   17.____
    way the government prevents one firm from dominating the market (c) a firm that engages in
    illegal activities (d) a perfectly competitive firm.

18. Monopolies (a) earn a profit (b) fail to earn a profit (c) break even (d) any of the previous   18.____

19. Which of the following is an example of perfect competition? (a) wheat (b) crude oil   19.____
    production (c) foreign exchange (d) all of the previous

20. Which of the following is an example of a commodity? (a) tennis shoes (b) soybeans (c) CD   20.____
    players (d) clothing

Part 3—Short Answer

Directions: Read the following questions, and write your response.

21. Why doesn't the farmer charge less than the market price for his agricultural goods?

22. Why is corn considered to be part of a perfectly competitive market structure?

Part 4—Critical Thinking

Directions: Read the following questions, and write your response.

23. Of the four market structures discussed in the chapter, which one or ones benefit consumers the most in
    terms of lowest prices and greatest product variety? Why? Provide at least one example of each market
    structure you discuss.

Lesson 8.1 Entrepreneurs

Part 1—True or False

Directions: Place a *T* for True or an *F* for False in the Answers column to show whether each of the following statements is true or false.

Answers

1. As long as an entrepreneur's business earns a profit in the short run, competitors and substitutes will naturally follow. 1._____

2. Entrepreneurs can improve people's standard of living. 2._____

3. An entrepreneur must turn an idea into a marketable product in order to earn a profit. 3._____

4. Because stockholders are not entrepreneurs, they do not accept the risk of a failing business. 4._____

5. The number of U.S. patents granted has decreased in recent decades. 5._____

6. A person is not considered an entrepreneur unless he or she invents a new product. 6._____

7. If someone copies a successful business, he or she can still be considered an entrepreneur. 7._____

8. Financial capital may be obtained from a bank. 8._____

9. The majority of businesses in the United States employ only one person. 9._____

10. Innovation is defined as the process of turning an invention into a marketable product. 10._____

Part 2—Multiple Choice

Directions: In the Answers column, write the letter that represents the word, or group of words, that correctly completes the statement or answers the question.

Answers

11. Which of the following is **not** true of an entrepreneur? (a) An entrepreneur looks for more efficient ways of doing things. (b) An entrepreneur seeks to make a profit. (c) An entrepreneur does not have to accept the risk of failure. (d) An entrepreneur may develop new products. 11._____

12. Rita invents a new flavor for popcorn. She writes a business plan, buys equipment, and finds buyers for her new product. Which of the following terms best describes Rita? (a) salaried worker (b) shareholder (c) entrepreneur (d) blue-collar worker 12._____

13. Which of the following is a true entrepreneur? (a) a stockholder in a large company (b) the founder of a company (c) an inventor who works for a large company (d) an inventor who gives over all power to a CEO 13._____

14. Which of the following terms is described as an inventor who works for a corporation? (a) entrepreneur (b) innovator (c) intrapreneur (d) venture capitalist 14._____

15. Which scenario is **not** considered a creative change that an entrepreneur might introduce into the market? (a) Abigail invents a new, less costly way to produce computers. (b) Bob opens a grocery-store chain that sells products similar to those sold by other chains. (c) Clara opens a fast-food chain that offers high-quality, gourmet burgers and fries. (d) David introduces a device that vacuums the entire house without the assistance of a human being. 15._____

16. Which of the following people may be considered a venture capitalist? (a) Lily gives money to Carl to help him start a business. (b) Lyle sells his house to raise the necessary funds to start his business. (c) Paul gets a bank loan for his new business. (d) all of the previous 16._____

17. Which of the following benefits from innovation? (a) the government (b) consumers   17._____
    (c) workers (d) all of the previous

18. Which of the following is an example of a business? (a) U.S. Airways opens a hub in another   18._____
    city. (b) A family of six opens a restaurant. (c) A 13-year-old earns money by shoveling his
    neighbors' driveways in the winter. (d) all of the previous

19. Entrepreneurs rely the most on ___?___ to indicate that business is successful. (a) profits   19._____
    (b) competitors (c) substitutes (d) prices of goods

20. ___?___ have the most influence on driving the economy forward. (a) Workers (b) Inventors   20._____
    (c) Entrepreneurs (d) Intrapreneurs

Part 3—Short Answer

Directions: Read the following questions, and write your response.

21. How can entrepreneurs finance their business ideas?

22. What differentiates the intrapreneur and the entrepreneur?

Part 4—Critical Thinking

Directions: Read the following questions, and write your response.

23. Provide a business example for each of the four types of creative changes made by entrepreneurs.
    (a) introduce new products (b) improve quality of existing products (c) introduce new production methods
    (d) introduce new ways of doing business

24. Why is the stockholder of a corporation not considered an entrepreneur even though there is risk of losing
    the investment?

25. The number of patents awarded to individuals fell from 22 percent to only 14 percent between 1980 and
    2000? (See Figure 8.1) What factors might have led to this reduction?

26. How do workers, consumers, and governments benefit by the contributions of entrepreneurs?

Name _____ Class _____ Date _____

Lesson 8.2   Sole Proprietorships and Partnerships

Part 1—True or False

Directions: Place a *T* for True or an *F* for False in the Answers column to show whether each of the following statements is true or false.

Answers

1. Real estate firms account for almost half of all partnerships.   1._____

2. Partnerships must be based on articles of partnership.   2._____

3. Limited partners do not have to share profits with anyone else.   3._____

4. By definition, all sole proprietorships have only one employee.   4._____

5. The sole proprietorship is the simplest form of business organization.   5._____

6. In a general partnership, each partner is personally responsible for paying all business debts.   6._____

7. A self-employed dentist is an example of a sole proprietor.   7._____

8. Liability is defined as the legal obligation to pay any debts of the business.   8._____

9. Most sole proprietors work in the agricultural industry.   9._____

10. A partnership must have two partners, at most.   10._____

Part 2—Multiple Choice

Directions: In the Answers column, write the letter that represents the word, or group of words, that correctly completes the statement or answers the question.

Answers

11. Which of the following people is the least liable in a business? (a) limited partner (b) sole proprietor (c) general partner (d) none of the previous   11._____

12. The word *limited* in limited partnership pertains to (a) the funds available to the partners (b) the partners' liability for loss should the company fail (c) the relatively small amount of taxes to be paid (d) the amount of managerial responsibility for each partner   12._____

13. Which of the following do sole proprietorships and partnerships share? (a) attract employees easily (b) allow founders complete control over the business (c) pay comparatively low taxes (d) have no difficulty raising large amounts of financial capital   13._____

14. Which of the following is a disadvantage of a partnership? (a) the life of the business is limited (b) disagreements between partners may arise (c) partners must share profits (d) all of the previous   14._____

15. Which of the following is true of a sole proprietorship? (a) The sole proprietor has complete control over business decisions. (b) The government heavily regulates sole proprietorships. (c) The sole proprietor must share profits with shareholders. (d) It is difficult to start up a sole proprietorship.   15._____

16. Which of the following is true of a partnership? (a) easy to start (b) worker retention is poor (c) government regulations are strict (d) difficult to raise even small amounts of financial capital   16._____

Part 3—Short Answer

Directions: Read the following questions, and write your response.

17. Name a few of the sole proprietorships located in your community.

18. How many businesses in the United States are sole proprietorships? What percentage of U.S. business sales are generated by sole proprietorships, and how many of them report sales of more than $1 million per year?

19. How many businesses were organized as partnerships in the year 2000? What percentage of business sales do they account for, and how many partnerships report sales of more than $1 million per year?

20. What are some of the reasons that sole proprietorships are the most common type of business organization?

21. What are some of the disadvantages of partnerships?

22. How is liability a drawback for sole proprietors and partnerships?

Part 4—Critical Thinking

Directions: Choose a business idea (restaurant, bowling alley, etc.) In the chart below, use the information you have learned to list advantages and disadvantages to organizing this business as a sole proprietorship or partnership.

23.

Sole Proprietorship		Partnership	
Advantages	**Disadvantages**	**Advantages**	**Disadvantages**

Lesson 〔8.3〕 Corporations and Other Organizations

Part 1—True or False

Directions: Place a *T* for True or an *F* for False in the Answers column to show whether each of the following statements is true or false.

Answers

1. A cooperative must pay government taxes on its profits.   1._____

2. It is not necessary for a not-for-profit organization to generate any income.   2._____

3. An LLC has more financial flexibility than an S corporation.   3._____

4. A corporation, but not the people who run it, can be sued.   4._____

5. S corporations tend to be comparatively small.   5._____

6. Owners of corporations have more control over business decisions than sole proprietors.   6._____

7. Corporations account for the majority of business sales.   7._____

8. Stockholders of a corporation must specialize in their company's business.   8._____

9. An existing partnership has the option of converting to a limited liability partnership.   9._____

10. The Red Cross is an example of a consumer cooperative.   10._____

Part 2—Multiple Choice

Directions: In the Answers column, write the letter that represents the word, or group of words, that correctly completes the statement or answers the questions.

Answers

11. Which is true of a publicly traded corporation? (a) Stocks can be bought and sold through a stock exchange. (b) There are only a handful of shareholders. (c) The majority of corporations are publicly traded corporations. (d) Stockholders rarely sell their stock.   11._____

12. A(n) ___?___ has both limited liability protection and single taxation. (a) private corporation (b) sole proprietorship (c) S corporation (d) publicly traded corporation   12._____

13. Which of the following are subjected to double taxation? (a) general partnerships (b) sole proprietorships (c) limited partnerships (d) corporations   13._____

14. Which of the following is **not** an example of a hybrid business? (a) publicly traded corporation (b) limited liability company (c) S corporation (d) limited liability partnership   14._____

15. If dairy farmers joined forces to buy equipment and market their products, into which category would their business fall? (a) consumer cooperative (b) S corporation (c) producer cooperative (d) limited liability partnership   15._____

16. Under which of the following categories do most private colleges fall? (a) not-for-profit organization (b) sole proprietorship (c) corporation (d) cooperative   16._____

17. What is the main difference between an S corporation and a limited liability company (LLC)? (a) An S corporation has limited liability while an LLC does not. (b) An S corporation cannot have any foreign investors while an LLC can. (c) An LLC is taxed only once while an S corporation is double taxed. (d) all of the previous   17._____

18. How does a limited liability partnership (LLP) differ from an LLC? (a) An LLC can have   18. _____
    foreign investors while an LLP cannot. (b) An LLP is taxed as a partnership while an LLC is
    not. (c) An LLC is taxed only once while an LLP is double taxed. (d) An LLP is easier to
    establish than an LLC.

Part 3—Short Answer

Directions: Read the following questions, and write your response.

19. How many corporations were organized in the United States in the year 2000? What percentage of all
    business sales did they account for? What was their median sales range?

20. What is the role of the board of directors?

21. What do shares of stock represent? What are dividends?

22. How do private and publicly traded corporations differ?

23. Explain the favorable circumstance of limited liability for stockholders.

24. How are corporations taxed twice?

Part 4—Critical Thinking

Directions: Read the following questions, and write your response.

25. Write a paragraph about the process of incorporating a sole proprietorship. What steps must be taken, and
    what are the advantages and disadvantages of the decision?

26. How can cooperatives reduce costs for consumers and producers?

Chapter ⑧ Review

Part 1—True or False

Directions: Place a *T* for True or an *F* for False in the Answers column to show whether each of the following statements is true or false.

Answers

1. A sole proprietor must share any profits with shareholders.   1. _____

2. An LLC can have foreign investors, but an S corporation cannot.   2. _____

3. An intrapeneur capitalist is an inventor who works for a corporation.   3. _____

4. Sole proprietorships always have higher tax rates than corporations.   4. _____

5. Entrepreneurs can tell if they are successful by examining their profits.   5. _____

6. The goal of a not-for-profit organization is to earn money for its shareholders.   6. _____

7. A sole proprietor is fully responsible for all the firm's losses.   7. _____

8. Owners of a corporation have the right to vote for the board of directors.   8. _____

9. A partnership faces many government regulations.   9. _____

10. Sole proprietorships are the most common type of business organization.   10. _____

Part 2—Multiple Choice

Directions: In the Answers column, write the letter that represents the word, or group of words, that correctly completes the statement or answers the question.

Answers

11. Bonnie hears about a new company that produces a new type of soft drink. She decides to   11. _____
buy stock in the company and makes arrangements through Todd, the CEO of the company.
Todd reports the news of the new shareholder to the Bob, the company's founder and Todd's
boss. Bob then calls to tell Monica, who works in the lab developing the new soft drink, the
good news. Who is an entrepreneur? (a) Bonnie (b) Todd (c) Bob (d) Monica.

12. Which of the following scenarios is not considered a creative change that an entrepreneur   12. _____
might introduce into the market? (a) Billy opens a home-improvement store that stocks the
same products as other home improvement stores. (b) Lily opens a pizza shop that allows
customers to make their own pizzas. (c) Shelly invents a new type of snow shovel. (d) Mica
invents a new, less costly way to manufacture dishwashers.

13. Who is a sole proprietor? (a) a private academic tutor (b) an employee of a coffee shop   13. _____
(c) a magazine salesperson (d) all of the previous

14. What is the first step in forming a corporation? (a) A charter is issued. (b) A corporation   14. _____
becomes a legal entity. (c) Articles of incorporation are determined to comply with the law.
(d) Articles of incorporation must be written.

15. Both sole proprietors and partnerships (a) pay comparatively low taxes (b) allow their   15. _____
founders limited control over business decisions (c) attract employees easily (d) have
difficulty raising large amounts of financial capital.

16. Under which category does the American Red Cross fall? (a) sole proprietorship (b) not-for-   16. _____
profit organization (c) corporation (d) cooperative

17. Maria, who knows nothing about manicures, makes financial contributions to her friend Amy's manicure business. Amy manages the day-to-day operations and has unlimited liability. Which term most accurately describes this business? (a) sole proprietorship (b) general proprietorship (c) limited partnership (d) none of the previous

17._____

18. Suppose wheat farmers join together to buy equipment for their farming needs. Under which category does this example fall? (a) S corporation (b) limited liability partnership (c) consumer cooperative (d) a producer cooperative.

18._____

19. Which of the following is a true entrepreneur? (a) a stockholder in a media company (b) a soda company's founder who gives all power to the CEO (c) the founder of a publishing company (d) an inventor who works for General Electric

19._____

Part 3—Short Answer

Directions: Read the following questions, and write your response.

20. Discuss the advantages and disadvantages of sole proprietorships.

21. Identify in the appropriate order the steps involved in forming a corporation.

Part 4—Critical Thinking

22. Suppose you and your friend decide to open a candy shop. Would it be best for you to form a general partnership or a limited partnership? Why? What advantages would there be in forming this partnership? Disadvantages? Explain.

Lesson ⬤9.1 Demand and Supply of Resources

Part 1—True or False

Directions: Place a *T* for True or an *F* for False in the Answers column to show whether each of the following statements is true or false.

Answers

1. A rightward shift in the demand for engineers increases their wage and the number of engineers employed.

   1._____

2. An increase in the price of oil increases the demand for coal.

   2._____

3. Technological improvements always shift the labor demand curve to the right.

   3._____

4. Firms are demanders in the resource market.

   4._____

5. A resource demand curve slopes downward.

   5._____

6. Productivity is defined as the demand for a resource that arises from the demand for the product that the resource produces.

   6._____

7. The market demand for electricity sums the demand for electricity as a means of producing light, heat, and all other uses.

   7._____

8. It is nearly impossible for firms to make substitutions in production.

   8._____

Part 2—Multiple Choice

Directions: In the Answers column, write the letter that represents the word, or group of words, that correctly completes the statement or answers the question.

Answers

9. If the price of a Chinese take-out meal increases, how would this affect the demand curve for Chinese chefs? (a) shifts rightward (b) shifts leftward (c) shifts downward (d) shifts upward

   9._____

10. If there is an increase in the demand for solar-powered cars, how would this affect the demand for automobile engineers? (a) demand would increase (b) demand would decrease (c) demand would remain constant (d) It cannot be determined from the information given.

    10._____

11. How would the supply for labor in an average working-class family be affected by a recession? Supply would (a) decrease (b) remain constant (c) increase (d) none of the previous

    11._____

12. What role do households most often play in the resource market? (a) demanders (b) suppliers (c) demanders and suppliers (c) none of the previous

    12._____

13. Which of the following would shift a labor supply curve? (a) working conditions for factory workers are improved (b) workers' tastes change so that jobs requiring physical labor become more popular (c) those suing tobacco companies are financially rewarded at the same time (d) all of the previous

    13._____

14. Which of these are resource substitutes? (a) peanuts and peanut butter (c) clothing and cotton (d) security system and security guards (d) computer consultants and computers

    14._____

15. Demand for a construction company derives from demand for (a) building tools (b) new buildings (c) construction workers (d) a construction site

    15._____

16. Which of the following results from achieving an equilibrium wage? (a) an excess quantity is demanded (b) an excess quantity is supplied (c) more is demanded than can be supplied (d) none of the previous

    16._____

17. If a new type of toothbrush were designed that cut down on the number of times a person should go to the dentist for cleanings, how would this affect the demand curve for dentists? (a) unaffected (b) shift rightward (c) shift leftward (d) shift upward

17._____

18. Why does the market supply curve slope upward? Resource suppliers are (a) more willing to supply a resource as its price increases (b) less able to supply a resource as its price increases (c) less willing to supply a resource as its price increases (d) none of the previous

18._____

Part 4—Critical Thinking

Directions: Read the following questions, and write your response.

19. How does a decrease in the price of gold affect the demand for jewelry designers (a resource complement)?

20. Relate the effect of personal wealth on the labor supply.

Part 5—Graphing

21. Graph the affect on teacher demand if new technology enables interactive delivery of college courses by the Internet.

22. Graph the affect of a prolonged stock market decline on the labor supply. What is the affect on wages and employment?

23. Graph and explain the affect of a large windfall of money on your future labor supply.

Lesson ⬤9.2 Wage Determination

Part 1—True or False

Directions: Place a *T* for True or an *F* for False in the Answers column to show whether each of the following statements is true or false.

Answers

1. Workers usually earn more per hour in seasonal jobs than in year-round jobs, other things constant.　　1._____

2. Workers represented by labor unions earn less on average than workers who do not belong to unions.　　2._____

3. The unemployment rate is highest for high-school dropouts.　　3._____

4. In March 2000, the president signed legislation increasing the minimum wage by $1.00 to $6.15.　　4._____

5. Costly job training increases market supply for a particular job.　　5._____

6. Education allows workers from every age group to earn more than uneducated workers.　　6._____

7. Differences in ability affect wages.　　7._____

8. Women now earn 100 percent of what men earn in the same job.　　8._____

Part 2—Multiple Choice

Directions: In the Answers column, write the letter that represents the word, or group of words, that correctly completes the statement or answers the question.

Answers

9. Which statement most accurately describes the relationship between education and income? (a) the more education, the lower the income (b) the more education, the higher the income (c) the less education, the higher the income (d) none of the previous　　9._____

10. Which of the following is **not** a factor that affects wages? (a) amount of education (b) amount of risk with a job (c) worker preferences on the job (d) discrimination　　10._____

11. How might an increase in the minimum wage affect the opportunity cost of staying in high school and graduating? The opportunity cost would (a) increase (b) decrease (c) not be affected (d) none of the previous　　11._____

12. Of the following people, who most likely earns the highest wage? (a) fast-food restaurant worker (b) coal miner (c) office assistant (d) filing clerk　　12._____

13. Which of the following are nonwage job components that an employer could change to offset the cost of a higher minimum wage? (a) on-the-job training (b) number of paid holidays (c) number of breaks (d) all of the previous　　13._____

14. Richard, a 47-year-old lawyer, mentors Julie, a 26-year-old lawyer who works in the same firm. Her father, Donald, also is 47 years old, but he works at a factory. He mentors Lily, a 25-year-old who works at the factory. Based on general trends and data discussed in the section, who earns the highest wage? (a) Lily (b) Julie (c) Donald (d) Richard　　14._____

15. How are wages affected as a worker ages? (a) increase (b) decrease (c) remain the same (d) none of the previous　　15._____

16. Which of the following best defines the purpose of the minimum wage law? (a) to guarantee 16.____
workers health insurance (b) to establish a minimum amount that an employer can pay a
worker for an hour of labor (c) to limit the amount of money that an employer pays a worker
for an hour of labor (d) none of the previous

17. Suppose the minimum wage increases by $.75. How might the owner of a small clothing shop 17.____
respond? (a) substitute part-time jobs for full-time jobs (b) substitute less-qualified workers for
more qualified minimum wage workers (c) take actions to decrease worker productivity
(d) take actions to increase employer costs

Part 3—Short Answer

Directions: Read the following questions, and write your response.

18. How does costly and lengthy training for a career reduce labor supply?

19. Why does a periodontist (root canal specialist) earn more than a dentist?

20. What factors affect earnings?

21. What are some explanations for the continued earnings gap between men and women?

Part 4—Critical Thinking

Directions: Read the following questions, and write your response.

22. Write a short description of the wage outlook of a career you are considering. Include training, education,
affects of age, experience, differences in abilities, degree of risk, geographic differences, and possible job
discrimination.

23. As a business owner of an urban restaurant franchise, how might an increase in minimum wage affect your
hiring practices?

24. During the heyday of the steel mill industry in Pittsburgh, PA, high-school graduates faced the decision of
stepping into full-time steel-mill positions at excellent rates of pay or attending college and working for a
decade to match the initial steel-mill pay. Explain the opportunity cost of choosing to attend college.

Lesson ⑨·³ Labor Unions

Part 1—True or False

Directions: Place a *T* for True or an *F* for False in the Answers column to show whether each of the following statements is true or false.

Answers

1. Union membership has decreased in recent years.   1. _____

2. Only the government may impose binding arbitration.   2. _____

3. Restrictions on imported goods can lead to an increased demand for union labor.   3. _____

4. More women than men belong to unions.   4. _____

5. Conditions in the workplace have improved dramatically, in part, due to unions.   5. _____

6. Unionization rates in right-to-work states are double the rates in other states.   6. _____

7. The highest membership rate for unions is for middle-aged males.   7. _____

8. The Taft-Hartley Act exempted labor unions from antitrust laws.   8. _____

9. A mediator may be brought in to enforce a decision regarding negotiations between union workers and the employer.   9. _____

10. Strikes usually benefit employers, not employees.   10. _____

Part 2—Multiple Choice

Directions: In the Answers column, write the letter that represents the word, or group of words, that correctly completes the statement or answers the questions.

Answers

11. How might unions go about increasing the wages of its members? (a) increase the supply of labor (b) decrease the demand for union labor (c) reduce the supply of labor (d) none of the previous   11. _____

12. Which of the following best defines the term "featherbedding"? (a) union efforts to require workers to join the union (b) union efforts to negotiate wages, employee benefits, and working conditions (c) union efforts to force employers to hire more workers than the task requires (d) union efforts to withhold labor from a firm   12. _____

13. Which of the following was established first? (a) Taft-Hartley Act (b) Clayton Act (c) Congress of Industrial Organizations (d) American Federation of Labor   13. _____

14. Which types of workers make up nearly half of all union members? (a) government workers (b) factory workers (c) construction workers (d) transportation workers   14. _____

15. How might a union restrict membership? (a) increase initiation fees (b) difficult qualification exams (c) shorter apprenticeship periods (d) all of the previous   15. _____

16. What resulted from the Congress of Industrial Organization (CIO)? (a) Union workers became organized by industries. (b) Only craftspeople were able to join unions. (c) States were authorized to approve right-to-work laws. (d) Labor unions became exempted from antitrust laws.   16. _____

17. Approximately what fraction of the workforce now belongs to a union? (a) one-fourth (b) one-third (c) one-seventh (d) one-half   17. _____

18. Which of the following might result from collective bargaining? (a) mediator called in   18. _____
(b) labor contract signed (c) strike occurs (d) all of the previous

19. Which of the following has reduced the power of unions in recent years? (a) increase in voters   19. _____
who belong to unions (b) the near disappearance of the strike (c) increase in employment in
the manufacturing sector (d) all of the previous

20. How might a union increase the demand for union labor? (a) increase the demand for union-   20. _____
made products (b) decrease union labor productivity (c) increase the supply of nonunion-made
products (d) all of the previous

Part 4—Critical Thinking

Directions: Read the following questions, and write your response.

21. Suppose workers in a unionized firm propose a job-sharing arrangement to the employer. Using the terms collective bargaining, mediator, binding arbitration, and strike, write a brief description of possible negotiations with the firm.

22. What appears to be the trend in union membership? Why?

Part 4—Graphing

23. Graph the effects of labor unions' intended goal to reduce the supply of labor and to increase the demand for union labor.

Chapter 9 Review

Part 1—True or False

Directions: Place a *T* for True or an *F* for False in the Answers column to show whether each of the following statements is true or false.

Answers

1. As a worker ages, his or her wage usually increases.   1._____

2. Featherbedding is defined as union efforts to force employers to hire more workers than are   2._____
   needed for the task.

3. The market supply curve slopes upward because resource suppliers are less able to supply a   3._____
   resource as its price increases.

4. A union is always aiming to increase membership.   4._____

5. Pharmacists earn different wages in different countries.   5._____

6. Union workers became organized by industries as a result of the Congress of Industrial   6._____
   Organization.

7. A mediator is an impartial observer who listens to both sides in a dispute and then suggests a   7._____
   solution that may or may not be used.

8. Technological improvements do not always shift the labor demand curve to the right.   8._____

9. The amount of risk associated with a job can have an effect on wages.   9._____

10. The purpose of the minimum wage law is to limit the amount of money that an employer pays   10._____
    a worker for an hour of labor.

Part 2—Multiple Choice

Directions: In the Answers column, write the letter that represents the word, or group of words, that correctly completes the statement or answers the question.

Answers

11. Of the following people, who is most likely to earn the lowest wage? (a) coal miner (b) lawyer   11._____
    (c) astronaut (d) administrative assistant

12. If the price of toilets decreases, how might this affect the demand curve for plumbers?   12._____
    (a) shift leftward (b) shift rightward (c) no affect (d) none of the previous

13. Which of the following are resource substitutes? (a) police officers and firefighters   13._____
    (b) furniture and lumber (c) automated factory robot and factory workers (d) engineers and
    construction workers

14. Linda is a 35-year-old tractor-trailer driver training Roberto, who is 31 years old. Naneeka,   14._____
    who is 26 years old, works in the tractor-trailer company's office. Her father, Malcolm, 52,
    founded the company. Based on general trends and data discussed in the textbook, who earns
    the highest wage? (a) Linda (b) Roberto (c) Naneeka (d) Malcolm

15. Which of the following affects wages? (a) level of education (b) discrimination (c) risk   15._____
    associated with job (d) all of the previous

16. The demand for carpenters derives from the demand for (a) cabinetry (b) electricians   16._____
    (c) lumber (d) nails

17. If the current wage rate is more than the equilibrium wage rate, there will be a (a) shortage of   17._____
    labor and wage rates will soon decrease (b) surplus of labor and wage rates will soon decrease
    (c) shortage of labor and wage rates will soon increase (d) surplus of labor and wage rates will
    soon increase

18. If the cost of machines that assemble automobiles automatically increases by 2 percent, the   18._____
    demand for workers who assemble automobiles by hand will probably (a) remain unchanged
    (b) decrease (c) increase (d) be eliminated

19. Randy, Jordan, Emilio, and Stephan are all 31-year-old attorneys in the same firm. On   19._____
    average, Randy works 60 hours a week; Jordan, 55; Emilio, 50; and Stephan, 40. Who most
    likely earns the highest wage? (a) Randy (b) Jordan (c) Emilio (d) Stephan

20. If there is a decrease in the demand for apartment housing, the demand for construction   20._____
    workers is likely to (a) increase (b) decrease (c) remain constant (d) It cannot be determined
    from the information given.

Part 3—Short Answer

Directions: Read the following questions, and write your response.

21. Suppose you are in the workforce for 40 years. How might your wage change over the course of that time
    period? Why? What other factors might affect your wage?

22. Suppose you work full time as a grocery clerk and earn minimum wage. How might your job be affected
    if the minimum wage is increased?

Part 4—Critical Thinking

23. Suppose you are a college mathematics professor and head the university's union. The union and the
    administration cannot reach a collective bargaining agreement. What are your options?

Lesson   10.1   Production, Consumption, and Time

Part 1—True or False

Directions: Place a *T* for True or an *F* for False in the Answers column to show whether each of the following statements is true or false.

Answers

1. Advanced industrial economies invest more than other economies.   1._____

2. Firms are the only demanders of loans.   2._____

3. The lower the interest rate, the greater the quantity of loans demanded.   3._____

4. An increase in capital makes workers more productive.   4._____

5. An interest rate is almost always below 5 percent.   5._____

6. In general, people value future consumption over present consumption.   6._____

7. Interest can be viewed as the reward for not consuming in the present.   7._____

8. The lower the interest rate, the less money someone will borrow.   8._____

9. Present consumption usually costs more than future consumption.   9._____

10. The demand curve for loans reflects a negative relationship between the interest rate and the   10._____
    quantity of loans demanded.

Part 2—Multiple Choice

Directions: In the Answers column, write the letter that represents the word, or group of words, that correctly completes the statement or answers the question.

Answers

11. Which of the following is true of the supply curve for loans? (a) It shows that the more people   11._____
    save, the fewer loans supplied. (b) The curve slopes downward. (c) The curve shifts rightward
    as the interest rate decreases. (d) It shows a positive relationship between interest rate and the
    quantity of loans supplied.

12. How much interest is charged annually if you borrow $850 at an 8 percent interest rate?   12._____
    (a) $8.50 (b) $16.25 (c) $68 (d) $85

13. Which of the following is absolutely essential to production? (a) savings (b) borrowers   13._____
    (c) investors (d) loans

14. Suppose you can buy a new style of corduroy pants the day they're put on store shelves. You   14._____
    also have the option of waiting a few weeks for the pants to go on sale or even waiting a few
    months for them to show up at the outlet stores. Which option would cost you the most
    money? (a) buying the pants after they've gone on sale (b) buying the pants at the outlet store
    (c) buying the pants the day stores put them on display (d) It cannot be determined from the
    information given.

15. Which situation illustrates that an equilibrium interest rate has been achieved? (a) The   15._____
    quantity of loans demanded is greater than the quantity of loans supplied. (b) The quantity of
    loans demanded is equal to the quantity of loans supplied. (c) The quantity of loans demanded
    is less than the quantity of loans supplied. (d) none of the previous

16. Who determines the market rate of interest? (a) those who demand loans (b) those who save money (c) those who supply loans (d) all of the previous 16._____

17. Why does the demand curve for loans slope downward? (a) because firms borrow more when the interest rate declines (b) because firms borrow less when the interest rate declines (c) because there is a positive relationship between interest rate and the quantity of loans demanded (d) none of the previous 17._____

18. Which of the following results from investment? (a) labor (b) capital goods (c) interest rates (d) none of the previous 18._____

19. Who is a key player in the market for loans? (a) savers (b) borrowers (c) suppliers (d) all of the previous 19._____

20. Suppose the interest rate for borrowing money from a bank increases. What effect would this have on the demand for loans curve? (a) rightward shift of the curve (b) movement along the curve (d) leftward shift of the curve (d) none of the previous 20._____

Part 3—Short Answer

Directions: Read the following questions, and write your response.

21. How might impatience affect a consumer's buying habits?

22. Why do home purchases increase when mortgage rates decline?

23. What are some typical items that households borrow to pay for?

Part 4—Critical Thinking

Directions: Read the following questions, and write your response.

24. How is the equilibrium, or market interest rate, determined?

25. How might expectations of future interest rates changes affect people's choices to save now?

Lesson ⬤10.2 Banks, Interest, and Corporate Finance

Part 1—True or False

Directions: Place a *T* for True or an *F* for False in the Answers column to show whether each of the following statements is true or false.

Answers

1. Interest rates are identical across all industries, e.g., car loans, home mortgages, personal loans.

   1._____

2. The secondary market for securities decreases the liquidity of securities.

   2._____

3. The interest earned on loans to state and local governments is not subject to federal income taxes.

   3._____

4. An initial public offering allows the public to buy stock in a company.

   4._____

5. The more valuable the collateral backing up a loan, the lower the interest rate charged on that loan.

   5._____

6. Bonds have outperformed stocks in every decade.

   6._____

7. As the duration of a loan increases, the interest rate charged decreases.

   7._____

8. All borrowers are guaranteed the prime rate.

   8._____

9. Owners of securities are never allowed to resell them.

   9._____

10. Interest rates are higher for loans that involve greater risks.

    10._____

Part 2—Multiple Choice

Directions: In the Answers column, write the letter that represents the word, or group of words, that correctly completes the statement or answers the question.

Answers

11. Suppose that four different firms take out four different loans as follows: Firm A: Loan amount of $1,000; Firm B: Loan amount of $25,000; Firm C: Loan amount of $8,020; Firm D: Loan amount of $20,600. Which firm's loan will have the lowest administration cost per dollar borrowed? (a) firm A (b) firm B (c) firm C (d) firm D

    11._____

12. How does a corporation acquire financial capital? (a) through retained earnings (b) by borrowing from banks (c) by issuing stock (d) all of the previous.

    12._____

13. Who is a financial intermediary? (a) saver (b) bank (c) borrower (d) the IRS

    13._____

14. Which of the following is a payment shareholders of a company receive? (a) retained earnings (b) bonds (c) dividends (d) securities

    14._____

15. Why might a business negotiate a line of credit with a bank? (a) so that the business can borrow money when and as it is needed (b) so that the business can open a savings account (c) so that a business can obtain a mortgage on its property (d) none of the previous

    15._____

16. If a corporation issues a bond, what is it promising to do? (a) pay back the holder a monthly fixed sum until the loan is completely paid off (b) pay back the holder a fixed sum of money on the maturity date plus annual interest (c) pay back the holder within a one-year period (d) pay back the holder at a given maturity date without paying interest.

    16._____

17. Why would a saver use a bank to lend money out instead of making loans directly to   17. _____
    borrowers? (a) Savers are unable to find borrowers without banks. (b) Savers need credit,
    which can only be gained through a bank. (c) Banks reduce the transaction costs of lending
    money to borrowers. (d) all of the previous

18. Which of the following is an example of securities? (a) retained earnings (b) dividends   18. _____
    (c) collateral (d) stocks

19. Which of the following terms is defined as the ability to borrow now based on the promise of   19. _____
    repayment in the future? (a) credit (b) prime rate (c) bond (d) line of credit

20. What is the market value of a firm on a given day if there are 600,000 shares outstanding at a   20. _____
    price of $4 per share? (a) $150,000 (b) $200,000 (c) $2,400,000 (d) $10,000,000

Part 3—Short Answer

Directions: Read the following questions, and write your response.

21. In what way do banks reduce the transaction costs between savers and borrowers?

22. Name a business that may need to access a line of credit for use during off seasons.

Part 4—Critical Thinking

Directions: Read the following questions, and write your response.

23. Write a short message to the public about how to avoid identity theft.

24. Describe how a borrower might secure the lowest possible interest rate considering risk, duration of the
    loan, costs and tax treatment.

Part 5—Graphing

25. Create a labeled graph depicting the market interest rate of loans at 5.7% for borrowers and savers. On
    your graph, show the effect an increase in household incomes would have on market interest rates.

Lesson ⬤10.3 Business Growth

Part 1—True or False

Directions: Place a *T* for True or an *F* for False in the Answers column to show whether each of the following statements is true or false.

Answers

1. Burger King is an example of a franchise.   1. _____

2. A merger between a clothing producer and a media company is an example of a conglomerate merger.   2. _____

3. Financial markets allocate funds readily to corporations experiencing financial difficulty.   3. _____

4. Firms grew quickly in the last half of the nineteenth century because the geographical size of markets increased.   4. _____

5. Franchises slow down the rate at which a business grows.   5. _____

6. The greater a corporation's profit, other things constant, the higher the value of the corporation's shares.   6. _____

7. With a conglomerate merger, one firm combines with another from which it buys inputs or to which it sells output.   7. _____

8. Mergers are the quickest way for a company to grow.   8. _____

9. The Third Merger Wave occurred between 1948 and 1969.   9. _____

10. The Fourth Merger Wave came to an end due to hostile takeovers.   10. _____

Part 2—Multiple Choice

Directions: In the Answers column, write the letter that represents the word, or group of words, that correctly completes the statement or answers the questions.

Answers

11. Of the following cities, where would an American multinational corporation most likely be based? (a) Los Angeles (b) Taiwan (c) Sydney (d) Barcelona   11. _____

12. What was the most prevalent type of merger during the Second Merge Wave? (a) horizontal mergers (b) vertical mergers (c) conglomerate mergers (d) all of the previous   12. _____

13. What is the advantage to buying a franchise? (a) the risk of failure is lower than if one opened a brand new business (b) people with limited experience can run a business (c) people gain valuable marketing and production experience (d) all of the previous   13. _____

14. Most of the world's largest multinational corporations are located in (a) Mexico City (b) the Netherlands (c) Europe (d) the United States   14. _____

15. Suppose a company that cuts trees to provide firms with timber merges with a construction company. What type of merger has occurred? (a) conglomerate merger (b) horizontal merger (c) input merger (d) vertical merger   15. _____

16. Which of the following contributed to the First Merger Wave (1887–1904)? (a) hostile takeovers (b) technological breakthroughs (c) an increase in the cost of transportation (d) all of the previous   16. _____

17. Why do profitable firms grow faster? (a) They can more easily obtain loans. (b) More profits can be given to shareholders. (c) Owners tend to invest less of their own money into the firm. (d) all of the previous   17._____

18. What caused the First Merger Wave to end? (a) hostile takeovers (b) conglomerate mergers (c) antitrust laws (d) the stock market crash   18._____

19. During which decade did the largest mergers in history occur? (a) 1930s (b) 1950s (c) 1990s (d) 1920s   19._____

20. Why did many of the conglomerate mergers of the Third Merger Wave fail? (a) results of the stock market crash and the Great Depression (b) hostile takeovers were out of control (c) firms tried to produce all types of products well instead of focusing on a few (d) too much competition in the market   20._____

Part 3—Short Answer

Directions: Read the following questions, and write your response.

21. How do high share values benefit a corporation?

22. What are some of the benefits of operating a franchise business?

23. What are some benefits to firms that operate as multinational corporations?

Part 4—Critical Thinking

Directions: Read the following questions, and write your response.

24. Summarize the types of mergers for each of the four merger waves. (a) 1887–1904 (b) 1916–1929 (c) 1948–1969 (d) 1982–2000

25. Why are some of the pro and con arguments of multinational influences in poorer countries?

Name _____ Class _____ Date _____

Chapter ⬤10 Review

Part 1—True or False

Directions: Place a *T* for True or an *F* for False in the Answers column to show whether each of the following statements is true or false.

Answers

1. When people save more and businesses borrow less, interest rates will increase.   1._____

2. Those who demand and supply loans determine the market rate of interest.   2._____

3. The higher the interest rate, the greater the quantity of loans demanded.   3._____

4. Profitable firms grow faster because they can more easily obtain loans.   4._____

5. Banks are an example of a financial intermediary.   5._____

6. Opening a franchise can increase the rate at which a firm can grow.   6._____

7. As a general trend, people value future consumption over present consumption.   7._____

8. During the 1980s many mergers were hostile, meaning they violated antitrust laws.   8._____

9. Interest rates differ across industries.   9._____

10. The supply curve for loans shifts rightward as the interest rate decreases.   10._____

Part 2—Multiple Choice

Directions: In the Answers column, write the letter that represents the word, or group of words, that correctly completes the statement or answers the question.

Answers

11. How much interest is charged if you borrow $2,000 at a 3 percent interest rate for one year?   11._____
    (a) $60 (b) $2,000 (c) $3 (d) $100

12. Which of the following is true about a bond? (a) The bondholder will pay back the issuer a   12._____
    fixed sum of money on the maturity date plus annual interest. (b) The bond's issuer will pay
    back the holder a fixed sum of money on the maturity date plus annual interest. (c) The bond's
    issuer will pay back the holder at a given maturity date without paying interest. (d) The
    bondholder will pay back the issuer within a one-year period

13. Of the following cities, where would an American multinational corporation most likely be   13._____
    based? (a) Atlanta (b) Mexico (c) London (d) Dublin

14. Suppose the interest rate for borrowing money from a bank decreases from 5 percent to 4.5   14._____
    percent. What effect would this have on the demand for loans curve? (a) shift rightward
    (b) shift leftward (c) movement along the curve (d) none of the previous

15. A company that assembles computers merges with a firm that makes circuits. What type of   15._____
    merger has occurred? (a) input merger (b) conglomerate merger (c) horizontal merger
    (d) vertical merger

16. Which of the following would most require savings? (a) preparing to produce corn   16._____
    (b) preparing to produce sandwiches (c) preparing to produce pizza (d) preparing to produce
    cat food

17. Suppose that firm A takes out a loan of $20,000; firm B takes out a loan of $25,000; firm C   17. _____
    takes out a loan of $2,000; and firm D takes out a loan of $35,000. Which firm has the lowest
    administration cost-per dollar borrowed? (a) firm A (b) firm B (c) firm C (d) firm D

18. Where might a multinational corporation most likely manufacture goods? (a) Los Angeles   18. _____
    (b) Taiwan (c) New York City (d) all of the previous

19. An example of a capital good would be (a) the machine you use at your factory job to produce 19. _____
    tires (b) the paper on which you write your essay (c) the bicycle on which you ride to school
    (d) all of the previous

20. What is the market value of a firm on a given day if there are 800,000 shares outstanding at a   20. _____
    price of $9 per share? (a) $88,888 (b) $1,000,000 (c) $7,200,000 (d) It cannot be determined
    from the information given.

Part 3—Short Answer

Directions: Read the following questions, and write your response.

21. Why are you willing to pay more for a hardcover book today than wait six months for the same book to
    come out in the lower-priced paperback edition?

22. Suppose you earn $2,000 over the course of a summer. Why might you choose to deposit this money into
    a bank?

Part 4—Critical Thinking

23. Suppose you decide to take out a loan from a bank. Provide two examples of items that could serve as your
    collateral. Provide one example of an item that would not be accepted as collateral and explain why. What
    would happen to the annual interest rate of your loan as the duration of the loan increased? Why?

Lesson ⬤ 11.1 Gross Domestic Product

Part 1—True or False

Directions: Place a *T* for True or an *F* for False in the Answers column to show whether each of the following statements is true or false.

Answers

1. Only nondurable goods are factored into consumption.

   1._____

2. GDP can be measured only through calculating total spending on U.S. production.

   2._____

3. The term "economy" may describe the structure of economic activity in a locality, region, country, group of countries, or the world.

   3._____

4. Unemployment compensation payments are not counted as government purchases.

   4._____

5. Spending by households on new residential construction is not considered investment.

   5._____

6. The value of U.S. imports has exceeded the value of U.S. exports nearly every year since the 1960s.

   6._____

7. The sum of the value added for all final goods and services equals GDP based on the income approach.

   7._____

8. Cars that have been produced but not yet sold can be considered inventory.

   8._____

9. GDP includes the value of second-hand goods.

   9._____

10. The value of services provided by realtors is not included in measuring GDP.

    10._____

Part 2—Multiple Choice

Directions: In the Answers column, write the letter that represents the word, or group of words, that correctly completes the statement or answers the question.

Answers

11. Which of the following is an example of a government purchase? (a) municipal trash collection (b) Social Security payments (c) automobile sales (d) airplane fares

    11._____

12. Which of the following would be considered an intermediate good? (a) new car purchased by a teenager (b) new computers purchased by an accounting business (c) ground beef purchased by McDonald's (d) toothpaste

    12._____

13. Which of the following best defines aggregate income? (a) the sum of all the income earned by resource suppliers in the economy during a given year (b) the total spending on all final goods and services produced in the economy during a given year (c) the purchase of new plants, new equipment, new buildings, new residences, and net additions to inventories (d) household purchases of final goods and services

    13._____

14. Suppose U.S. investment is $50,000,000 and consumption is $70,000,000. Government purchases total $30,000,000 while exports are $60,000,000 and imports are $80,000,000. What is the aggregate expenditure? (a) $100,000,000 (b) $130,000,000 (c) $170,000,000 (d) $290,000,000

    14._____

15. Which of the following is the most common way to measure an economy's size? (a) the number of people employed (b) gross product (c) the value of all goods sold (d) people's total income

    15._____

16. Which of the following is a nondurable good? (a) furniture (b) a stereo (c) cheese (d) a truck   16._____

17. The expenditure approach to GDP takes which of the following into account? (b) investment   17._____
    (b) government purchases (c) consumption (d) all of the previous

18. Which of the following spending components changes the most from year to year?   18._____
    (a) investment (b) consumption (c) government purchases (d) net exports

19. Suppose you buy a piece of pottery for your mother for $100. In order to produce that piece   19._____
    of pottery, a firm had to dig for clay. This raw clay was sold for $10. Another firm processed
    the clay and sold it to a potter for $15. The potter created the pottery from the clay and sold it
    to a local shop for $70. You bought the pottery from this shop. What is the market value of
    the final good? (a) $70 (b) $95 (c) $100 (d) $195

20. Which of the following would **not** be included in measuring U.S. GDP? (a) how much an   20._____
    American company produces in its Malaysian plant (b) how much is produced by an
    American-owned company located in Ohio (c) how much is produced by a Japanese
    company located in California (d) none of the previous

Part 3—Short Answer

Directions: Read the following questions, and write your response.

21. Why does the GDP exclude foreign production by a General Motors plant in Mexico?

22. What do national income accounts track?

Part 4—Critical Thinking

Directions: Read the following questions, and write your response.

23. Name and describe an intermediate good that may be purchased during the production of a dining room
    table.

24. Explain the negative net export balance component of the GDP.

25. Contrast aggregate income and GDP.

26. Use the following example to explain the "value added" concept and how it is reflected in GDP. Jim's
    deli pays $.90 for turkey, $.30 for cheese, $.15 for the roll, $.08 for mayonnaise and $.10 for lettuce. Jim
    sells the turkey sandwich for $4.50.

Lesson ⬤ 11.2 Limitations of GDP Estimation

Part 1—True or False

Directions: Place a *T* for True or an *F* for False in the Answers column to show whether each of the following statements is true or false.

Answers

1. Household production typically is not measured in GDP.

   1. _____

2. GDP typically captures all features of the economy that contribute to standard of living.

   2. _____

3. Older capital may be less valuable as a productive resource due to wear and tear.

   3. _____

4. Net domestic product does not account for the value of the capital stock used up in the production process.

   4. _____

5. GDP measures the value of output in current dollars.

   5. _____

6. Real GDP allows you to make meaningful comparisons of GDP across years.

   6. _____

7. A price index is constructed by multiplying each year's price by the price in the base year, and then multiplying the result by 100.

   7. _____

8. The consumer price index (CPI) is used to identify changes in the "cost of living."

   8. _____

9. In order to compute the GDP price index, you need to know both nominal GDP and real GDP.

   9. _____

10. The base year that the federal government uses to compute real GDP moves forward from time to time.

    10. _____

Part 2—Multiple Choice

Directions: In the Answers column, write the letter that represents the word, or group of words, that correctly completes the statement or answers the question.

Answers

11. If net investment is positive, we can assume capital stock (a) remains fixed (b) grows (c) declines (d) none of the previous

    11. _____

12. Which of the following best defines green accounting? (a) GDP that accounts for production in the underground economy (b) GDP that measures depreciation (c) GDP that reflects the impact of production on pollution to the environment (d) GDP that takes innovations and improvements into account

    12. _____

13. Suppose Country A is composed of households that are largely self-sufficient. Country B's households specialize and sell products to one another. Assuming that these countries have similar populations and productive capabilities, which of the following statements is probably true? (a) Country A's GDP is less than Country B's GDP. (b) Country A's GDP is greater than Country B's GDP. (c) Country A's GDP is equal to Country B's GDP. (d) It cannot be determined from the information given.

    13. _____

14. Suppose you want to determine U.S. GDP for the year 1972. You want to ensure that the figure has been adjusted to reflect inflation. Which of the following would you consider? (a) inflation GDP (b) real GDP (c) nominal GDP (d) none of the previous

    14. _____

15. Which of the following does GDP ignore? (a) the amount of money spent in building an office complex (b) the earnings of a paid housekeeper (c) the amount of money people spend on housing purchases (d) the value of the work performed by a couple that does its own cleaning and cooking

    15. _____

16. What is the GDP price index if real GDP is $15,000,000 and nominal GDP is $30,000,000?   16.____
    (a) 100 (b) 200 (c) 50 (d) 75

17. What does the consumer price index measure? (a) nominal GDP (b) real GDP (c) changes in   17.____
    costs of goods and services over time (d) depreciation

18. Which of the following is **not** included in GDP? (a) changes in the quality of existing products   18.____
    (b) the availability of new products (c) the amount of leisure time available to the average
    worker (d) all of the previous

19. After researching the price of orange juice in a variety of years, you gather the following data: 19.____
    in 1960 the price of orange juice was $1.00; in 1961 the price was $1.05; in 1962 it was $1.09;
    and in 1963 the price was $1.19. If 1960 is the base year, what was the price index of orange
    juice in 1962? (a) 100 (b) 109 (c) 91 (d) 118

20. A price index (a) permits price comparisons between any two years (b) compares nominal and   20.____
    real GDP (c) always takes depreciation of capital stock into account (d) measures production
    in the underground economy.

Part 3—Short Answer

Directions: Read the following questions, and write your response.

21. What types of production are omitted in the GDP?

22. What are some of the activities that represent the underground market or activities not disclosed for
    taxation?

23. What happens to the economy's capital stock if net investment is (a) negative (b) zero (c) positive?

24. How does the CPI measure inflation?

Part 4—Critical Thinking

Directions: Read the following questions, and write your response.

25. What is true about leisure time in the United States today compared to 100 years ago?

26. What is green GDP and how do you predict this information might be used in the future?

Lesson   **11.3**   Business Cycles

Part 1—True or False

Directions: Place a *T* for True or an *F* for False in the Answers column to show whether each of the following statements is true or false.

                                                                                                          Answers

1. Expansions typically last longer than recessions.   1._____

2. No two business cycles are identical.   2._____

3. Recessions affect regions around the country in identical ways.   3._____

4. Recessions can be identified only after their onset.   4._____

5. The index of leading indicators is made up of 15 items.   5._____

6. Leading indicators are so accurate that they always predict when a turning point in the economy will occur.   6._____

7. Business cycles in a given country usually affect those of other countries.   7._____

8. A drop in production during a particular quarter almost always results in a shock to the economy.   8._____

9. Leading indicators are especially applicable when there is an external shock to the economy.   9._____

10. Economists consider personal income to be a coincident indicator.   10._____

Part 2—Multiple Choice

Directions: In the Answers column, write the letter that represents the word, or group of words, that correctly completes the statement or answers the question.

                                                                                                   Answers

11. A media report that industrial production has decreased would be considered a(n) ___?___ indicator? (a) lagging (b) leading (c) coincident (d) premeditative   11._____

12. If Japan's economy experienced an expansion, what would you expect to happen in the United States? (a) The U.S. economy would experience a depression. (b) The U.S. economy would experience a recession. (c) The U.S. economy would experience an expansion. (d) The U.S. economy would not be affected.   12._____

13. Which of the following is included in the index of lagging indicators? (a) interest rate (b) average duration of unemployment (c) measures of loans outstanding (d) all of the previous   13._____

14. How long must a deep contraction in the economy last to be considered a depression? (a) six months (b) two consecutive quarters (c) more than a year (d) eighteen months   14._____

15. Suppose Region A produces corn, Region B produces electronic equipment, Region C produces dairy products and Region D produces beef. Which region would be hit the hardest by a recession? (a) region A (b) region B (c) region C (d) region D   15._____

16. How has the GDP generally changed through the last 80 years? (a) increased (b) decreased (c) remained relatively fixed (d) none of the previous   16._____

17. Which term is defined as the period between a high point and a low point in an economy?   17._____
    (a) peak (b) recession (c) trough (d) expansion

18. Production increases in the long run because there are (a) decreases in the amount of labor   18._____
    (b) decreases in the amount of capital (c) improvements in technology (d) increases in sales

Part 3—Short Answer

Directions: Read the following questions, and write your response.

19. What is the difference between a recession and a depression?

20. List a leading indicator and a lagging indicator of the business cycle.

Part 4—Fill in the Blank

Directions: In the space provided, write the word or phrase that best completes each statement.

21. In a business cycle, the period between a trough and a peak is known as a(n) _____.

22. The period between a peak and a trough is known as a(n) _____.

23. The average growth rate of the U.S. economy since 1929 has been _____ per year.

Part 5 —Critical Thinking

Directions: Read the following questions, and write your response.

24. What are some of the characteristics represented in the U.S. economy during record expansionary period in the 1990s?

25. What would be the best time in regard to the business cycle for an entrepreneur to start a business?

Part 6—Graphing

26. **Directions:** Label the four parts of the business cycle below. Place an H where high levels of employment are likely. Place a U where low levels of employment are likely.

_____

Lesson ⬤11.4 Aggregate Demand and Aggregate Supply

Part 1—True or False

Directions: Place a *T* for True or an *F* for False in the Answers column to show whether each of the following statements is true or false.

Answers

1. Real GDP demanded decreases as U.S. price levels increase.   1._____

2. The vertical axis of an aggregate demand curve measures real GDP.   2._____

3. Wage rates typically are assumed to remain constant along the aggregate supply curve.   3._____

4. Greater levels of real GDP along the aggregate supply curve usually translate into fewer people who are employed.   4._____

5. On the aggregate demand curve, quantity of output demanded is inversely related to the price level, other things constant.   5._____

6. The aggregate supply curve slopes downward.   6._____

7. Real GDP had an average annual growth rate of 3.4 percent from 1929 to 2002.   7._____

8. The best measure of aggregate output is nominal GDP.   8._____

9. The United States produces a greater value of goods and services than any other economy in the world.   9._____

10. Real GDP results from adjusting GDP for price changes.   10._____

Part 2—Multiple Choice

Directions: In the Answers column, write the letter that represents the word, or group of words, that correctly completes the statement or answers the question.

Answers

11. The aggregate supply curve reflects what type of relationship between price level and the quantity of aggregate output that producers supply? (a) negative relationship (b) direct relationship (c) inverse relationship (d) none of the previous   11._____

12. What occurs at the point in which the aggregate demand curve and the aggregate supply curve intersect? (a) quantity demanded is greater than quantity supplied (b) quantity demanded is less than quantity supplied (c) equilibrium is achieved (d) none of the previous   12._____

13. Which of the following has increased since 1929? (a) workers' average level of education (b) worker productivity (c) the number of workers (d) all of the previous   13._____

14. Which of the following best describes the relationship reflected by the aggregate demand curve? (a) direct relationship (b) inverse relationship (c) independent relationship (d) none of the previous   14._____

15. Which of the following is considered constant when examining a given aggregate demand curve? (a) real GDP (b) price levels in the United States (c) price levels in other countries (d) nominal GDP   15._____

16. Which of the following is reflected in the aggregate demand curve? (a) price level and real   16.____
    GDP demanded (b) price level and nominal GDP demanded (c) real GDP and nominal GDP
    demanded (d) none of the previous

17. Which of the following is **not** considered to be constant along an aggregate supply curve?   17.____
    (a) prices of resources (b) the state of technology (c) exchange rates between the U.S. dollar
    and foreign currencies (d) the rules of the game that provide production incentives

18. Aggregate demand sums the demands of which of the following decision makers? (a) firms   18.____
    (b) households (c) governments (d) all of the previous

Part 3—Short Answer

Directions: Read the following questions, and write your response.

19. Who are the four economic decision makers that account for aggregate demand?

20. What happens to the amount of aggregate demand as the price level decreases?

Part 4—Critical Thinking

Directions: Read the following questions, and write your response.

21. How is the economy able to provide employment for additional workers as population grows over time?

22. Determine real GDP per capita in an economy with a $60 billion dollar real GDP and a population of 20
    million.

Part 5—Graphing

23. **Directions**: Construct an aggregate demand and aggregate supply curve meeting at an equilibrium price
    level of $9 trillion. Draw new curves on the graph that show what would happen to the locations of
    aggregate demand and supply if the government reduced personal income taxes while it also increased
    taxes on imported natural resources. What would happen to the price level in the economy?

_____

Chapter ⓫ Review

_____

Part 1—True or False

Directions: Place a *T* for True or an *F* for False in the Answers column to show whether each of the following statements is true or false.

Answers

1. Gross product is the most common way to measure an economy's size.　　　　　1._____

2. A measure of loans outstanding is not included in the index of lagging indicators.　　2._____

3. The consumer price index is a measure of inflation.　　　　　3._____

4. Unemployment compensation payments are counted as government purchases in GDP.　4._____

5. Production increases in the long run because there are usually improvements in technology.　5._____

6. The aggregate supply curve reflects an inverse relationship between price level and the quantity of aggregate output that producers supply.　　6._____

7. Real GDP provides a more accurate picture of the economy than nominal GDP.　　7._____

8. The expenditure approach to measuring GDP only takes consumption into account.　8._____

9. Recessions affect regions around the country in different ways.　　9._____

10. GDP always measures the value of output in real dollars.　　10._____

Part 2—Multiple Choice

Directions: In the Answers column, write the letter that represents the word, or group of words, that correctly completes the statement or answers the question.

Answers

11. What is the GDP price index if real GDP is $20,000,000 and nominal GDP is $50,000,000?　11._____
    (a) 40 (b) 100 (c) 150 (d) 250

12. Suppose the media reports that the average household income has increased. What type of　12._____
    indicator does this information represent? (a) coincident indicator (b) lagging indicator
    (c) leading indicator (d) limiting indicator

13. Which term represents a period between a trough and a peak? (a) expansion (b) recession　13._____
    (c) depression (d) none of the above

14. An example of an intermediate good is (a) a song from a CD that is sold separately as a single　14._____
    (b) ground beef you buy at the grocery store (c) chicken sold to Kentucky Fried Chicken
    (d) train tracks

15. After researching the price of a loaf of bread in a variety of years, you gather the following　15._____
    data: In 1925, a loaf of bread cost $.10; in 1926, $.13; in 1927, $.15; and in 1928, $.17. If
    1925 is the base year, what is the price index for a loaf of bread in 1927? (a) 100 (b) 130
    (c) 150 (d) 200

16. Which of the following is a nondurable good? (a) an automobile (b) antibiotic medications　16._____
    (c) a refrigerator (d) carpeting for your living room

Name _____ Class _____ Date _____

17. If the United Kingdom's economy experienced a recession, Japan's economy would most likely (a) experience an expansion (b) experience a recession (c) experience a depression (d) would not be affected

17._____

18. Which of the following will be counted as part of GDP? (a) the value of your work to shovel snow off your driveway (b) the sale of a used car produced in 1999 (c) the preparation of a take-out meal that will be consumed this evening (d) the processing of a beam of lumber that will be used to build a house

18._____

19. Which of the following is reflected in the aggregate demand curve? (a) nominal GDP demanded and price level (b) real GDP and nominal GDP demanded (c) price level and price index (d) real GDP demanded and price level

19._____

20. Which of the following would be included in measuring U.S. GDP? (a) how much is produced by a Mexican company located in Mexico (b) how much is produced by a Japanese company located in Florida (c) how much is produced by a Dutch company located in France (d) how much an American company produces in its Taiwanese plant

20._____

21. Which of the following best defines aggregate demand? (a) a composite measure reflecting the prices of all goods and services in the economy relative to prices in a base year (b) the relationship between the economy's price level and the quantity of aggregate output demanded, other things constant (c) a composite measure of all final goods and services produced in an economy during a given period (d) none of the previous

21._____

22. Real GDP per capita is a measure of which of the following? (a) how much an economy produces on average per resident (b) how much an economy produces on average per year (c) how much an economy produces on average per household (d) how much an economy produces on average per capital good

22._____

Part 3—Short Answer

Directions: Read the following questions, and write your response.

23. Explain the difference between the aggregate expenditure approach to calculating GDP and the income approach.

24. Provide three examples of things that are not included in calculating GDP.

Lesson ⬤12.1 The PPF, Economic Growth, and Productivity

Part 1—True or False

Directions: Place a *T* for True or an *F* for False in the Answers column to show whether each of the following statements is true or false.

Answers

1. For the most part, land productivity determines the standard of living in the United States today.   1. _____

2. A stable political climate would promote investment in the economy.   2. _____

3. The amount of capital produced this year would rarely affect the location of the PPF in the next year.   3. _____

4. An improvement in technology usually expands the PPF.   4. _____

5. Labor accounts for a relatively small portion of the cost of production.   5. _____

6. Most growth comes from increases in the quantity of resources.   6. _____

7. Economists study the productivity of all resources, including labor, capital, and land.   7. _____

8. Capital deepening is the only source of rising labor productivity.   8. _____

9. Labor is the resource most commonly used to measure productivity because it can be measured easily.   9. _____

10. The greater the productivity, the more goods and services can be produced from a given amount of resources.   10. _____

Part 2—Multiple Choice

Directions: In the Answers column, write the letter that represents the word, or group of words, that correctly completes the statement or answers the question.

Answers

11. Which of the following is an example of physical capital? (a) construction worker (b) milk (c) doughnut (d) highway   11. _____

12. What effects might changes in the rules of the game have on economic growth? (a) expands (b) contracts (c) not affected (d) all of the previous   12. _____

13. If an economy invests more in capital this year, what will most likely happen to the amount of consumer goods that are consumed in that same year? (a) increase (b) decrease (c) not be affected (d) It cannot be determined from the information given.   13. _____

14. Which of the following illustrates capital deepening? (a) The CEO of a company decides to hire only those candidates with a college degree in business (b) The owner of a factory cuts back on the amount of employees he will hire. (c) The publisher of a newspaper invests in new, more up-to-date computers for her staff. (d) The government decreases the amount of taxes that certain companies must pay.   14. _____

15. What do points inside the production possibilities frontier (PPF) represent? (a) inefficient combinations of consumer goods and capital goods (b) unattainable combinations of consumer goods and capital goods (c) the quantity of capital goods produced if all the economy's resources are employed efficiently to produce them (d) the quantity of consumer goods produced if all the economy's resources are employed efficiently to produce them   15. _____

16. People are encouraged to undertake productive activity through (a) customs (b) laws (c) conventions (d) all of the previous   16. _____

17. What would most likely happen to the PPF of a given company if it suddenly loses most of its capital stock in a fire? (a) the PPF would be unaffected (b) the PPF would shift outward (c) the PPF would shift inward d) none of the previous   17. _____

18. Which of the following best defines the phrase "standard of living"? (a) the level of economic prosperity enjoyed by people (b) output per unit of labor (c) manufactured creations used to produce goods and services (d) an increase in the quantity and quality of capital per worker   18. _____

19. Suppose it takes a knitter eight hours to produce one scarf. What is the knitter's labor productivity per hour of labor? (a) 8 (b) 1 (c) 0.125 (d) 0.502   19. _____

20. Which of the following situations would stimulate economic growth? (a) Patent laws are made more stringent. (b) A new invention allows paper producers to create more paper using fewer trees. (c) The population decreases suddenly as a result of an outbreak of a virus. (d) all of the previous   20. _____

Part 3—Short Answer

Directions: Read the following scenario, and write your response.

21. Name some of the factors that could cause an economy's production possibilities curve to shift outward?

22. How does an economy's production possibilities curve illustrate opportunity cost?

23. How are labor productivity and standard of living related?

24. What has enabled many economies to grow despite having limited land or infertile land?

Part 4—Critical Thinking

Directions: Read the following questions, and write your response.

25. How has the human and physical capital improved over the years in the field of food production?

26. What evidence of capital deepening do you see happening in the United States?

Lesson ⬤12.2 Living Standards and Labor Productivity Growth

Part 1—True or False

Directions: Place a *T* for True or an *F* for False in the Answers column to show whether each of the following statements is true or false.

Answers

1. If labor productivity remained unchanged, real GDP would still grow if the quantity of labor increased.   1._____

2. Today the American population is more educated (has completed more years of school) than any other national population in the world.   2._____

3. Only a small percentage of adults from industrial market economies are illiterate.   3._____

4. Higher labor productivity growth cannot make up for output lost during recessions.   4._____

5. United States citizens enjoy one of the highest standards of living in the world.   5._____

6. There has been a general upward trend in real GDP per capita for the United States since 1959.   6._____

7. Total output can grow as a result of greater labor productivity, but not more labor.   7._____

8. Technological developments have increased real output per work hour.   8._____

9. The Group of 7 represents countries that are considered developing.   9._____

10. Most of the world is comprised of developing countries.   10._____

Part 2—Multiple Choice

Directions: In the Answers column, write the letter that represents the word, or group of words, that correctly completes the statement or answers the question.

Answers

11. Which of the following is not a member of the Group of 7? (a) New Zealand (b) France (c) Italy (d) Germany   11._____

12. What is the best measure of an economy's standard of living? (a) the average salary per household (b) output per capita (c) real GDP (d) none of the previous   12._____

13. Which of the following statements is true about developing countries? (a) Developing countries have a great deal of human capital but not physical capital. (b) The farming methods used by farmers in developing countries are quite advanced. (c) Most of the workers in developing countries work in agriculture. (d) Labor productivity in developing countries is high.   13._____

14. Which of the following economies has produced more output per capita than any other major economy? (a) the United States (b) the United Kingdom (c) Japan (d) Germany   14._____

15. What allows economists to worry less about short-term fluctuations in output related to the business cycle and more about long-term growth? (a) advances in technology (b) the cumulative power of productivity growth (c) the poor productivity growth of foreign countries (d) all of the previous   15._____

16. What is the key to a rising standard of living? (a) an increase in spending (b) an increase in   16. _____
    exports (c) growth in labor productivity (d) all of the previous

17. What percentage of the world's countries is considered developed? (a) 80% (b) 50% (c) 20%   17. _____
    (d) 1%

18. Why did the rate of growth in labor productivity from 1974 to 1982 slow down so much?   18. _____
    (a) a number of laws designed to protect the environment were passed (b) a sharp increase in
    energy prices fueled inflation (c) the combination of three recessions slowed productivity
    growth (d) all of the previous

19. Which of these is **not** an industrial market country? (a) Canada (b) Australia (c) Japan   19. _____
    (d) Honduras

Part 3—Fill in the Blank

Directions: In the space provided, fill in the statistics about world standards of living.

20. Industrialized countries make up _____ percent of the world's population. Developing
    countries make up _____ percent.

21. More than _____ percent of workers in developing countries work in agriculture. In the United
    States, only_____ percent of all workers are in agriculture.

22. Per capita output in the United States is more than _____ times that of the world's poorest
    countries.

Part 4—Short Answer

Directions: Read the following questions, and write your response.

23. What is the correlation between developed countries and education?

24. Why has output per capita grown faster than labor productivity since 1959?

Part 5—Critical Thinking

Directions: Read the following questions, and write your response.

25. What conclusions can be drawn about growth in productivity from the graph on p. 369? What predictions
    might be made about the 2000 decade?

26. Refer to the graph on page 371. In the late 1999 recession, GDP did not contract until after the recession
    began. What might account for this?

Lesson ⬤12.3 Issues of Technological Change

Part 1—True or False

Directions: Place a *T* for True or an *F* for False in the Answers column to show whether each of the following statements is true or false.

Answers

1. Research has shown that employment levels today are lower than they were in the nineteenth century.

    1. _____

2. Defense technologies have become less important to U.S. industrial policy since the demise of the Soviet Union.

    2. _____

3. A hardware store chain that has stores located around the country is an example of a cluster.

    3. _____

4. R&D spending by governments and nonprofits is more likely for applied research.

    4. _____

5. Traditionally Japan has had the most aggressive policy for regulating and supporting favored industries.

    5. _____

6. Technological change may cause individual hardships in the short run.

    6. _____

7. Employment levels in economies where the latest technology has not yet been introduced are lower than those in economies who use the latest technology.

    7. _____

8. Investment in R&D reflects the economy's efforts to improve productivity through technological discoveries.

    8. _____

9. The United States devotes relatively more resources to R&D than most other advanced economies.

    9. _____

10. Worker productivity has decreased throughout the past 100 years.

    10. _____

Part 2—Multiple Choice

Directions: In the Answers column, write the letter that represents the word, or group of words, that correctly completes the statement or answers the questions.

Answers

11. Which of the following is a long-term effect of new technology? (a) lower productivity (b) higher real incomes (c) decreased standard of living (d) less leisure time

    11. _____

12. Why would a given firm want to form a cluster? (a) so that it could be the only firm of its kind in a particular area (b) to avoid competition (c) to increase cooperation between cluster members (d) to form its own customer base

    12. _____

13. Which of the following is an example of applied research? (a) Scientists invent a food additive that would help protect people in Third World Countries from polio. (c) Scientists attempt to measure how much heat a bolt of lightening emits. (b) Researchers conduct experiments to determine how worms reproduce. (d) Researchers study how World War II affected the number of births in the United States.

    13. _____

14. Which country's businesses had the lowest research and development spending in the 1990s? (a) Italy (b) Japan (c) the United States (d) none of the previous

    14. _____

15. Which of the following is true about the effects of technological breakthroughs? (a) products   15. _____
    may become more affordable (b) production may increase (c) some workers may lose their
    jobs (d) all of the previous

16. What is the objective of U.S. industrial policy? (a) to secure a leading global role for U.S.   16. _____
    industry (b) to ensure adequate investment in research (c) to promote investment in particular
    industries (d) all of the previous

17. How is research and development spending tracked? (a) by examining it in relation to the   17. _____
    unemployment rate (b) by examining it in relation to output per capita (c) by examining it in
    relation to GDP (d) none of the previous

18. Critics of industrial policy justify their skepticism by (a) claiming that markets allocate scarce   18. _____
    resources better than governments do (b) pointing to research that shows industrial policy
    decreases productivity (c) say clusters will form too aggressively (d) all of the previous

Part 3—Short Answer

Directions: Read the following scenario, and write your response.

19. Why is the payoff less immediate with basic research than with applied research?

20. How does R&D improve productivity?

21. What is the advantage of an industry cluster?

Part 4—Critical Thinking

Directions: Read the following questions, and write your response.

22. As improved technologies decrease the number of workers needed in many industries, what will keep the
    unemployment rate from rising over the long run?

23. What could be some of the advantages or disadvantages of a government's industrial policy?

24. What advice might you offer to a new worker in today's workforce to increase chances of employability
    over the course of the person's career?

Chapter ⑫ Review

Part 1—True or False

Directions: Place a *T* for True or an *F* for False in the Answers column to show whether each of the following statements is true or false.

Answers

1. As productivity increases, the amount of goods and services produced from a given amount of resources decreases.   1. _____

2. The United States has produced more output per capita than any other major economy.   2. _____

3. Standard of living is defined as the level of economic prosperity people enjoy.   3. _____

4. The best measure of an economy's standard of living is real GDP.   4. _____

5. An increase in spending raises a country's standard of living.   5. _____

6. The more stable an economy is, the more investment there is likely to be.   6. _____

7. Developing countries have a great deal of human capital but not physical capital.   7. _____

8. The quality of labor is the resource most responsible for increasing labor productivity.   8. _____

9. Labor accounts for a very large portion of the cost of production.   9. _____

10. Research and development spending is tracked by examining it in relation to GDP.   10. _____

Part 2—Multiple Choice

Directions: In the Answers column, write the letter that represents the word, or group of words, that correctly completes the statement or answers the question.

Answers

11. When labor productivity grows, it usually (a) grows at different rates for different workers (b) grows at the same rate for all workers (c) grows at an increasing rate over time (d) grows at a decreasing rate over time   11. _____

12. A(n) ___?___ is not an example of physical capital. (a) screwdriver (b) accountant (c) sheet of plywood (d) kitchen sink.   12. _____

13. A distinguishing feature between industrial economies and developing economies is the __?__ of the population. (a) gender (b) size (c) family structure (d) literacy   13. _____

14. ___?___ is the resource most responsible for increasing labor productivity. (a) Experience (b) Education (c) Capital (d) Aptitude   14. _____

15. Which of the following people would be a displaced worker? (a) a ski instructor who is laid off after ski season (b) a factory worker who is replaced by a new machine (c) a sales clerk who is laid off during a recession (d) a recent college graduated who has not yet found a job   15. _____

16. Suppose it takes a seamstress twelve hours to produce two dresses. What is this worker's labor productivity per hour? (a) 0.167 (b) 1 (c) 6 (d) 1.67   16. _____

17. When compared to other major economies, the United States produced ___?___ output per capita in 2000. (a) the most (b) the least (c) about the same (d) a smaller rate of   17. _____

18. Which of these countries is an industrial market country? (a) Honduras (b) Kashmir (c) Japan   18. _____
    (d) Cuba

19. Which of the following is an example of basic research? (a) a new metal alloy for use in golf   19. _____
    clubs is developed (b) another solar system is discovered (c) a new way to convert soybeans
    into automobile fuel is found (d) a new computer operating system is developed

Part 3—Short Answer

Directions: Read the following questions, and write your response.

20. What are rules of the game? How do they affect productivity?

21. Explain the difference between basic research and applied research, providing an example for each.

Part 4—Critical Thinking

22. In the space provided below, define an industry cluster, and discuss its advantages and disadvantages.

23. What are some examples of existing rules of the game that impede progress in the world?

Lesson ⬤13.1 Unemployment

Part 1—True or False

Directions: Place a *T* for True or an *F* for False in the Answers column to show whether each of the following statements is true or false.

Answers

1. Unemployment benefits may increase the average length of unemployment and the unemployment rate.

   1. _____

2. The majority of all unemployed workers receive unemployment benefits.

   2. _____

3. The unemployment rates in different areas of the country usually are identical.

   3. _____

4. A person who is just entering the workforce does not qualify for unemployment benefits.

   4. _____

5. There is frictional, structural, and seasonal unemployment even in a healthy, growing economy.

   5. _____

6. Frictional unemployment does not usually last for a long period of time.

   6. _____

7. Cyclical unemployment decreases during expansions.

   7. _____

8. Unemployment rates are higher among teenagers than among those over age 20.

   8. _____

Part 2—Multiple Choice

Directions: In the Answers column, write the letter that represents the word, or group of words, that correctly completes the statement or answers the question.

Answers

9. What condition must be fulfilled in order for an economy to be considered at full employment? (a) unemployment rate is zero (b) no structural unemployment (c) no cyclical unemployment (d) no seasonal unemployment

   9. _____

10. What is considered the true loss associated with unemployment? (a) fewer goods and services are produced (b) the unemployed person may suffer a loss of self-esteem (c) families of the unemployed suffer because of the lack of income (d) all of the previous

    10. _____

11. Why might unemployment figures be underestimated? (a) Some of those working in the underground economy are counted as unemployed. (b) The figures ignore discouraged workers who have dropped out of the labor force. (c) Those who do not really want a job but are seeking financial assistance from government transfer programs, which require them to be actively seeking employment, are counted as unemployed. (d) all of the previous

    11. _____

12. Someone who is unemployed can qualify for unemployment benefits if he or she (a) is actively seeking a new job (b) earned a certain amount of money at the previous place of employment (c) reports his or her weekly expenses to government officials (d) all of the previous

    12. _____

13. Which of the following people are **not** qualified to receive unemployment benefits? (a) a woman who quit her last job (b) a man who was unjustly fired from his last job (c) a woman who was laid off (d) a man who lost his job during cutbacks resulting from a recession

    13. _____

Name _____ Class _____ Date _____

14. Suppose that there are 300,000 people who are unemployed while there are 3,500,000 people   14. _____
    in the labor force. What is the unemployment rate (expressed as a percentage)? (a) 0.08%
    (b) 1.5% (c) 8.6% (d) 11.7%

15. Which of the following scenarios is an example of underemployment? (a) A woman with a   15. _____
    college degree in drama works as a waitress. (b) An apprentice to a carpenter is hired by
    another carpenter. (c) A man with the appropriate license works as an emergency medical
    technician. (d) A woman who has been trained as a secretary is promoted to buyer in a
    clothing company.

Part 3—Matching

Directions: Match the following type of unemployment to the corresponding example. (A) frictional
unemployment, (B) structural unemployment, (C) seasonal unemployment, (D) cyclical unemployment

Answers

16. Due to the decrease in demand for new cars, John was let go from his job at General   16. _____
    Motors.

17. Due to the number of factories moving overseas, Bob finds his tool and dye skills   17. _____
    outdated in today's economy.

18. Rita left her teaching job in California behind to seek her dream job with an art gallery   18. _____
    in New York City.

19. Jeanne's job as a master ski instructor leaves her without work from May until October   19. _____
    each year.

Part 4—Critical Thinking

Directions: Read the following questions, and write your response.

20. Provide an example of how a discouraged worker, an underemployed worker, and a worker in the
    underground economy can skew the unemployment estimates.

21. Calculate the labor-force participation rate for the town of Homeville, which has a noninstitutional adult
    population of 450,000 and 255,000 people who are employed or looking for work.

22. What might be some reasons for higher than average unemployment rates for teens ages 16–19 years?

Lesson 13.2 Inflation

Part 1—True or False

Directions: Place a *T* for True or an *F* for False in the Answers column to show whether each of the following statements is true or false.

Answers

1. The United States experienced hyperinflation during the Great Depression.
    1. _____

2. Stagflation occurs when price decreases and real GDP increases.
    2. _____

3. There has been a nine-fold increase in the consumer price index since 1946.
    3. _____

4. Since the end of World War II, the consumer price index has increased on a yearly basis (on average).
    4. _____

5. There is only one cause of inflation.
    5. _____

6. The price level was lower in 1940 than in 1920.
    6. _____

7. Inflation increases confidence in the value of the dollar over the long term.
    7. _____

8. Other things constant, the higher the expected inflation rate, the higher the nominal rate of interest that lenders require.
    8. _____

9. To generate sustained and continuous cost-push inflation, the aggregate supply curve would have to keep shifting to the left along a given aggregate demand curve.
    9. _____

10. It is quite easy to predict how inflation will behave.
    10. _____

Part 2—Multiple Choice

Directions: In the Answers column, write the letter that represents the word, or group of words, that correctly completes the statement or answers the question.

Answers

11. If the inflation rate is 7.7% and the nominal interest rate is 9%, what is the real interest rate?
    (a) 1% (b) 1.3% (c) 16.7% (d) It cannot be determined from the information given.
    11. _____

12. Unexpected inflation may result in which of the following for a given firm? (a) decrease in the real cost of union labor (b) increase in the effectiveness of long term plans (c) transaction costs of market exchange decrease (d) all of the previous
    12. _____

13. An increase in aggregate demand causes what type of inflation? (a) hyperinflation (b) demand-pull inflation (c) disinflation (d) cost-push inflation
    13. _____

14. What does the consumer price index measure? (a) cost of a specific consumer good over time (b) cost of a specific consumer service on a particular day (c) cost of all consumer goods over time (d) cost of a "market basket" of consumer goods and services over time
    14. _____

15. If inflation turns out to be different from what is expected, who benefits the most? (a) the person who had agreed to sell at a price that anticipated lower inflation (b) the person who had agreed to pay a price that anticipated higher inflation (c) the person who had agreed to pay a price that anticipated lower inflation (d) none of the previous
    15. _____

16. Which of the following measures interest in terms of current dollars? (a) the inflation rate (b) the nominal interest rate (c) the real interest rate (d) all of the previous
    16. _____

Part 3—Short Answer

Directions: Read the following questions, and write your response.

17. What does the annual inflation rate measure?

18. What is the difference between hyperinflation and disinflation?

Part 5—Critical Thinking

Directions: Read the following questions, and write your response.

19. If wages rise accordingly, is annual inflation necessarily bad for an economy?

20. If people are willing and able to pay a higher price for a good, what differentiates price gouging from increased demand?

21. How can inflation affect productivity internationally?

22. If the nominal interest rate on a four-year car loan is 6.2%, and inflation averages 3.5% over the loan term, what is the real interest rate?

Part 6—Graphing

Directions: Graph the following inflationary circumstance.

23. A four-year drought greatly affects crop production in the Midwest and western United States.

Lesson 13.3 Economic Instability

Part 1—True or False

Directions: Place a *T* for True or an *F* for False in the Answers column to show whether each of the following statements is true or false.

Answers

1. Stagflation creates higher unemployment and higher inflation. 1._____

2. Federal budget deficits steadily worsened during the 1990s. 2._____

3. The Keynesian approach may be thought of as supply-side economics. 3._____

4. Before the Great Depression, the government interfered a great deal in the market economy. 4._____

5. The 1960s was considered to be the golden age of Keynesian economics. 5._____

6. The laissez-faire doctrine holds that the government should not intervene in a market economy 6._____
   beyond the minimum required to maintain peace and property rights.

7. Inflation rose sharply during the late 1960s due to an increase in federal spending. 7._____

8. Demand-side economics was effective in combating stagflation. 8._____

9. John Maynard Keynes proposed that the government should not become involved in the 9._____
   economy.

10. During the 1980s, demand-side policies fixed economic problems and maintained a healthy 10._____
    economy.

Part 2—Multiple Choice

Directions: In the Answers column, write the letter that represents the word, or group of words, that correctly completes the statement or answers the question.

Answers

11. Which of the following best defines stagflation? (a) an expansion in the economy's aggregate 11._____
    output combined with a rise in the economy's price level (b) a contraction in the economy's
    aggregate output combined with a rise in the economy's price level (c) an expansion in the
    economy's aggregate output combined with a decrease in the economy's price level (d) a
    contraction in the economy's aggregate output combined with a decrease in the economy's
    price level

12. Demand-side economics promotes which of the following actions? (a) shifting the aggregate 12._____
    demand curve (b) creating new jobs (c) relying on natural forces to improve the economy
    (d) none of the previous

13. How did the Great Depression affect the aggregate demand curve? (a) curve shifted right 13._____
    (b) curve shifted left (c) leftward movement along the curve (d) curve was unaffected

14. How does supply-side economics stimulate aggregate supply? (a) by increasing the interest 14._____
    rate (b) by changing aggregate demand (c) by cutting taxes (d) all of the previous

15. What resulted from the Great Depression? (a) price level increased (b) real GDP increased 15._____
    (c) unemployment increased (a) all of the previous

16. What did the Employment Act of 1946 require the government to do? (a) foster maximum   16._____
    production (b) appoint a Council of Economic Advisers (c) The president must report annually
    on the state of the economy. (d) all of the previous

17. With which of the following statements would John Maynard Keynes most likely agree?   17._____
    (a) There are no natural market forces operating to ensure that an economy will return to a
    higher level of output and employment. (b) Aggregate demand is stable. (c) Investment
    decisions are quite predictable. (d) Businesses will most likely increase investment spending if
    they are pessimistic about the economy.

18. What conditions do economists think led to the Great Depression? (a) the 1929 stock market   18._____
    crash (b) restrictions on world trade (c) a drop in consumer spending (d) all of the previous

19. Stagflation occurred in which decade? (a) 1920s (b) 1930s (c) 1950s (d) 1970s   19._____

20. Which of the following actions did President Ronald Reagan take? (a) decreased sales taxes   20._____
    (b) increased personal income taxes for the rich (c) cut personal income tax rates (d) none of
    the previous

Part 4 —Critical Thinking

Directions: Read the following questions, and write your response.

21. How did the era of Keynesian demand-side economics build the national debt?

22. Summarize the economic circumstances of the 1970s known as stagflation.

23. Why did the tax cuts of supply-side economics not lead to a balanced budget?

Part 5—Graphing

24. **Directions:** Create a graph that depicts an increase in aggregate supply. What affect will this have on the price
    unemployment, and GDP?

Lesson (13.4) Poverty

Part 1—True or False

Directions: Place a *T* for True or an *F* for False in the Answers column to show whether each of the following statements is true or false.

Answers

1. The poverty rate and the unemployment rate have a direct relationship. 1._____

2. Research indicates that daughters from welfare families are not any more likely than daughters from non-welfare families to participate in the welfare system themselves. 2._____

3. Economists have not found any negatives relating to the welfare system. 3._____

4. Today the average never-married mother is on welfare for a decade. 4._____

5. Welfare benefits decline as income from other sources increases. 5._____

6. Poverty rates are higher across the upper half of the United States. 6._____

7. Between 1995 and 2001, the number of welfare recipients fell by more than half. 7._____

8. The poverty rate is about four times greater in families with no workers than in families with at least one worker. 8._____

9. Many unemployed people are discouraged from getting a job because for each additional dollar they earn, the higher their taxes will be. 9._____

10. The most direct way the government can help reduce poverty is to increase the amount of time people may remain on welfare. 10._____

Part 2—Multiple Choice

Directions: In the Answers column, write the letter that represents the word, or group of words, that correctly completes the statement or answers the question.

Answers

11. Of the following states, which has the highest poverty rate? (a) Massachusetts (b) Ohio (c) Louisiana (d) Maine 11._____

12. What might a person who has been on welfare for many years experience upon reentering the job force? (a) an increase in productivity (b) pay that is lower than that of their previous job (c) an increase in job skills (d) all of the previous 12._____

13. What is the best predictor of whether or not a family is poor? (a) the level of education achieved by the parents (b) the financial status of the father's parents (c) whether or not someone in the family collects unemployment insurance (d) whether or not someone in the family has a job 13._____

14. What is the cycle of poverty? (a) Children of welfare parents will inevitably be on welfare themselves. (b) Dependency on welfare from generation to generation cannot be avoided. (c) Children in welfare families have a greater chance of ending up on welfare when they are older. (d) Poverty affects all people in one neighborhood. 14._____

15. Which is the largest group living in poverty? (a) women (b) children (c) men (d) the elderly 15._____

16. Of all welfare recipients, economists have found that how many remain on welfare for at least eight years? (a) about a third (b) about ten percent (c) about a half (d) almost all   16._____

17. Which of the following reduces the poverty rate? (a) a high unemployment rate (b) a large number of people collecting unemployment insurance (c) a higher interest rate (d) none of the previous   17._____

18. Why might welfare recipients not want to find a job? (a) The government makes them repay benefits they have received in the past if they do so. (b) Many times the money and other benefits they receive from welfare are greater than what they could earn at a job. (c) They must remain on welfare for a certain period of time, or they will lose all benefits. (a) all of the previous   18._____

19. What did the overhaul of the welfare system in 1996 do? (a) require that the welfare recipient look for a job (b) impose a welfare limit of five years per recipient (d) require that the welfare recipient participate in training programs (d) all of the previous   19._____

20. Which of the following people have the greatest chance of living in poverty? (a) a family with two parents (b) a young, single mother (c) a young, single father (d) a family with grandparents raising the grandchildren   20._____

Part 3—Short Answer

Directions: Read the following question, and write your response.

21. How is the unemployment rate related to poverty?

22. What accounts for the higher poverty rates across the bottom half of the United States?

23. In what way can the welfare system discourage employment and self-sufficiency?

Part 4—Critical Thinking

Directions: Read the following question, and write your response.

24. Propose a plan for public education to help break the poverty cycle.

Name _____ Class _____ Date _____

Chapter ⬤13 Review

Part 1—True or False

Directions: Place a *T* for True or an *F* for False in the Answers column to show whether each of the following statements is true or false.

Answers

1. Inflation increases the value of money.   1._____
2. Demand-side economics promotes relying on natural forces to improve the economy.   2._____
3. The economy is considered to be at full employment when there is no structural   3._____
   unemployment.
4. The aggregate demand curve shifts leftward when the economy experiences cost-push   4._____
   inflation.
5. Inflation is an increase in the economy's price level resulting from a decrease in aggregate 5._____
   demand or an increase in aggregate supply.
6. An increase in aggregate demand causes demand-pull inflation.   6._____
7. Unemployment rates differ throughout sections of the United States.   7._____
8. Supply-side economics stimulates aggregate supply by cutting taxes.   8._____
9. Women are the largest group living in poverty.   9._____
10. Cyclical unemployment increases during expansions.   10._____

Part 2—Multiple Choice

Directions: In the Answers column, write the letter that represents the word, or group of words, that correctly completes the statement or answers the question.

Answers

11. During the Great Depression, the aggregate demand curve (a) remained constant (b) shifted to   11._____
    the left (c) shifted to the right (d) turned upside down.
12. If the inflation rate is 8% and the nominal interest rate is 5%, what is the real interest rate? 12._____
    (a) 13% (b) 8% (c) 5% (d) 3%
13. Which of the following people are qualified to receive unemployment benefits? (a) a man who 13._____
    was laid off (b) a man who quit his last job (c) a young woman who just graduated from
    college (d) all of the previous
14. Which of the following workers is seasonally unemployed? (a) a factory worker is laid off   14._____
    (b) a math tutor does not have the skills to help a student taking calculus (c) a fisherman
    cannot find work during the winter months (d) a nurse quits his job to go back to school
15. The nominal interest rate measures (a) interest in terms of current dollars (b) interest in terms 15._____
    of real dollars (c) the prime interest rate (d) interest in terms of real GDP
16. If there are 27,000 people who are unemployed, while there are 2,000,000 people in the labor 16._____
    force, what is the unemployment rate? (a) 7.4% (b) 27% (c) 1.35% (d) 13%

17. Which of the following situations illustrates structural unemployment? (a) A college student   17.____
    works at a grocery store over her summer vacation. (b) A computer consultant is not hired for
    a job because he is not familiar with a new computer program. (c) A truck driver is laid off due
    to an economic recession. (d) A woman makes a career change and takes six months off to
    look for a job.

18. The Employment Act of 1946 imposed a clear responsibility on the federal government to   18.____
    encourage (a) welfare reform (b) maximum employment, production, and purchasing power
    (c) investment (d) interest rate decreases

19. Which of the following is a result of inflation? (a) increases the value of the dollar over the   19.____
    short term (b) increases the value of the dollar over the long term (c) takes away confidence in
    the value of the dollar over the long term (d) increases confidence in the value of the dollar
    over the short term

20. What did the welfare reform of 1996 accomplish? (a) require that welfare recipients look for   20.____
    jobs (b) ban any limits as to how long an individual could receive welfare benefits (c) require
    the government to pay for recipients' job training (d) all of the previous

Part 3—Short Answer

Directions: Read the following questions and write several sentences in response.

21. Why is unexpected inflation more harmful than expected inflation? Explain.

22. Define supply-side economics. What is its goal?

Part 4—Critical Thinking

23. Write a paragraph that discusses the advantages and disadvantages of income assistance. How do you think
    the government should handle families living in poverty?

Lesson 14.1 Public Goods and Taxation

Part 1—True or False

Directions: Place a *T* for True or an *F* for False in the Answers column to show whether each of the following statements is true or false.

Answers

1. The government has the authority to impose fines on individuals or firms that pollute the environment.   1._____

2. User fees are similar to prices for private goods except that the fees often are more than the cost of the actual good or service.   2._____

3. Income tax rates are progressive.   3._____

4. The federal government relies primarily on the individual income tax for its revenue. 4._____

5. High marginal tax rates increase people's incentives to work, save, and invest.   5._____

6. Governments can cover a deficit by borrowing from the public.   6._____

7. A public good is rival in consumption.   7._____

8. The efficient level of a public good can be found by examining the point at which the neighborhood demand curve intersects the marginal cost curve.   8._____

9. Benefits-received taxation is the fairest way to tax people.   9._____

10. The ability-to-pay tax principle focuses more on a taxpayer's benefit from a public good than the taxpayer's income.   10._____

Part 2—Multiple Choice

Directions: In the Answers column, write the letter that represents the word, or group of words, that correctly completes the statement or answers the question.

Answers

11. On which of the following do local governments rely? (a) user fees (b) property taxes (c) fines (d) all of the previous   11._____

12. Suppose a bill is introduced that would require all American citizens to pay 1 percent of their income to a new program that supports adult literacy programs. What type of taxation is the bill proposing? (a) proportional (b) progressive (d) incidence (d) regressive   12._____

13. What is the marginal tax rate? (a) the tax rate at which each household must pay for schools (b) the percentage of each additional dollar of income that goes to pay the tax (c) the rate that determines who actually bears the burden of a tax (d) none of the previous   13._____

14. For which of the following projects would a government be most likely to borrow money from households and firms? (a) a new shopping mall (b) increases in salary for government officials (c) an airport (d) all of the previous   14._____

15. Which of the following requires that the percentage of income paid in taxes decreases as income increases? (a) progressive (b) marginal (c) regressive (d) proportional   15._____

16. Sin taxes would be applied to which of the following products? (a) fast food (b) alcoholic beverages (c) automobiles (d) vacations   16._____

Part 3—Short Answer

Directions: Read the following scenario, and write several sentences in response.

17. What differentiates a public good from a private good?

18. What determines an efficient level of a public good?

19. Why is tuition at a public university considered to be a user fee?

Part 4—Fill in the Blank

Directions: Fill in the correct revenue source.

20. The federal government relies most on revenue from _____ taxes.
21. State governments rely most on taxes from _____ and _____taxes.
22. Local government relies most on _____ taxes.

Part 5—Critical Thinking

Directions: Read the following questions, and write your response.

23. What are some examples of the *free rider* problem, which occurs when people try to benefit from a public good without paying for it or by paying less than they think it is worth.

24. How are sin taxes an example of the benefits-received tax principle?

25. Regressive taxes are sometimes said to favor the rich. Explain.

26. What would be some advantages and disadvantages of a proportional tax system for federal income tax?

Name _____ Class _____ Date _____

Lesson   **14.2**   Federal, State, and Local Budgets

Part 1—True or False

Directions: Place a *T* for True or an *F* for False in the Answers column to show whether each of the following statements is true or false.

Answers

1. In most years the federal government spends more than it takes in and makes up the difference by borrowing from the public.   1._____

2. The U.S. federal budget is now more than $2 trillion a year.   2._____

3. By 2004, most federal spending shifted from income redistribution to defense.   3._____

4. The government does not fund higher education.   4._____

5. All states impose a general sales tax.   5._____

6. One of the effects of World War II was to boost the federal governments' spending.   6._____

7. The Sixteenth Amendment originally affected only the richest households.   7._____

8. The federal government created policies that were designed to stabilize the economy before the Depression.   8._____

9. The Federal Insurance Contributions Act refers to payroll taxes.   9._____

10. Property taxes do not affect you if you rent your home.   10._____

Part 2—Multiple Choice

Directions: In the Answers column, write the letter that represents the word, or group of words, that correctly completes the statement or answers the question.

Answers

11. What does the Sixteenth Amendment allow the government to tax? (a) personal income (b) property (c) alcohol purchases (d) housing   11._____

12. Local government spends most of its money on which of the following? (a) environment (b) housing (c) education (d) police   12._____

13. The state spends most of its funds on which of the following? (a) prisons (b) welfare (c) state police (d) schools   13._____

14. Why did government outlays in the world economy decrease relative to GDP between 1993 and 2003? (a) defense spending increased in many countries (b) market economies were poor, prompting governments to take action (c) private markets became more popular than socialist economies, thereby lessening the role of governments (d) all of the previous   14._____

15. Which of the following is true about a government budget? (a) usually specifies a one-year period (b) plan for government outlays (c) plan for government revenues (d) all of the previous   15._____

16. Payroll taxes do **not** support which of the following? (a) Medicaid (b) Social Security (c) Medicare (d) none of the previous are supported by payroll taxes   16._____

17. What is the largest source of state revenue? (a) sales tax (b) the federal government (c) state income tax (d) user fees   17._____

18. How has government spending as a share of GDP changed since 1929? (a) decreased by half (b) doubled (c) tripled (d) no change   18._____

19. What is the largest source of local revenue? (a) property tax (b) state and federal aid (c) user fees (d) none of the previous   19._____

20. What is the government's primary source of federal revenue? (a) tariffs on exports (b) tax on food stuffs (c) donations (d) personal income tax   20._____

Part 3—Short Answer

Directions: Read the following questions, and write your response.

21. Name a responsibility for each level of government.

Federal	
State	
Local	

22. How has the percentage of spending changed for defense between 1960 and 2004?

23. How has government spending as a percent of GDP changed since 1929?

24. What percentage of the federal budget paid the interest payments on the federal debt in 2004?

25. What are the two largest state expenditures?

Part 5—Critical Thinking

Directions: Read the following questions and your response.

26. How is today's federal income tax different from its inception in 1913?

27. What could be a reason for the doubling of payroll taxes since 1960?

28. Which countries have the largest government expenditures as a percentage of GDP?

Lesson 14.3 Economics of Public Choice

Part 1—True or False

Directions: Place a *T* for True or an *F* for False in the Answers column to show whether each of the following statements is true or false.

Answers

1. All goods and services financed by the government are also produced by the government.

1._____

2. Voters in the United States usually elect representatives to voice their views on government issues.

2._____

3. There is a bigger payoff in making wise public choices than private ones.

3._____

4. In public choice, each person gets one vote, regardless of income.

4._____

5. Government bureaus receive a great deal of consumer feedback and, as a result, constantly are able to improve.

5._____

6. The actions of government agencies often directly conflict with one another.

6._____

7. Political action committees are not permitted to donate money to congressional campaigns.

7._____

8. The cost to the typical voter of acquiring and acting on information about elected officials' proposals usually is greater than any possible benefit.

8._____

9. Certain laws that are in place to prevent elected representatives from catering to special interest groups have eliminated this problem completely.

9._____

10. If you personally object to a government program, you can prevent your taxes from supporting it.

10._____

Part 2—Multiple Choice

Directions: In the Answers column, write the letter that represents the word, or group of words, that correctly completes the statement or answers the questions.

Answers

11. Which of the following is **not** an example of a bureau? (a) the FBI (b) the Environmental Protection Agency (c) the Pentagon (d) the President's office

11._____

12. What is an acceptable way for voters to express their dissatisfaction with local government? (a) refuse to pay their taxes (b) ignore public officials until their term is complete (b) move into another jurisdiction (d) all of the previous

12._____

13. What is rational ignorance? (a) Most voters don't think it's worth the effort to keep up with elected officials' proposals. (b) Elected officials ensure that their proposals are kept confidential. (c) People make a conscious decision not to vote in order to protest certain proposals. (d) all of the previous

13._____

14. Goods and services financed by the government, such as garbage collection and highways, (a) must be produced by government workers only (b) must be produced only by private firms (c) can be produced by government workers and/or private firms (d) none of the previous

14._____

15. What does the theory of maximizing political support dictate? (a) All Americans must belong to a political party. (b) Firms support politicians who will pass laws to increase their profitability. (c) Elected representatives campaign to win as many votes and financial contributions as possible. (d) none of the previous

15._____

16. Why might legislatures prefer dealing with bureaus rather than with firms? (a) bureaus are more responsive to legislature's concerns (b) bureaus prevent legislators from rewarding political supporters with government jobs (c) bureaus provide superior goods and services (d) none of the previous   16._____

17. When governments contract with private firms to produce public goods and services, they are using ___?___ to supply the product. (a) the bureaucracy (b) the market (c) agencies (d) households   17._____

Part 3—Short Answer

Directions: Read the following questions, and write your response.

18. How many separate governments exist in the United States?

19. What do government representatives usually look to maximize?

20. How do PACs influence Congress?

21. What are bureaus?

Part 4—Critical Thinking

Directions: Read the following questions, and write your response.

22. Why does legislation often favor producers rather than consumers?

23. At what point does rational ignorance become an issue of concern for taxpayers?

24. Why is "voting with one's feet" not always practical.

Chapter (14) Review

Part 1—True or False

Directions: Place a *T* for True or an *F* for False in the Answers column to show whether each of the following statements is true or false.

Answers

1. The largest source of state revenue is state income tax.   1._____

2. Local governments rely completely on property taxes.   2._____

3. Elected representatives often cater to special interests rather than the public interest.   3._____

4. Progressive taxation means that the percentage of income paid in taxes increases as income increases.   4._____

5. Legislatures prefer dealing with private firms over bureaus because private firms are more responsive to their concerns.   5._____

6. A flat tax is proportional.   6._____

7. The marginal tax rate determines how much each household should contribute to school taxes.   7._____

8. The role of a bureau is to pass legislation.   8._____

9. Local government spends most of its money on education.   9._____

10. A public good is nonrival in consumption.   10._____

Part 2—Multiple Choice

Directions: In the Answers column, write the letter that represents the word, or group of words, that correctly completes the statement or answers the question.

Answers

11. Regressive taxes require that (a) the percentage of income paid in taxes increases as income increases (b) the percentage of income paid in taxes decreases as income increases (c) the percentage of income paid in taxes is the same for all citizens (d) everyone is rich   11._____

12. Suppose curbside recycling by a private company costs $55 per week. How much would a bureau be most likely to charge for curbside recycling? (a) $55 (b) $100 (c) less than $55 (d) $56   12._____

13. An example of a bureau is (a) the Environmental Protection Agency (b) the president's cabinet (c) the local school board (d) the mayor   13._____

14. Suppose a bill is introduced that would require all residents of Ohio to pay 0.6% of their income to a new welfare program. What type of taxation is the bill proposing? (a) incidence (b) proportional (c) regressive (d) progressive   14._____

15. Which of the following is an example of an ability-to-pay principle tax? (a) a sales tax on a chocolate bar (b) a sales tax on automobiles (c) the federal tax on income (d) all of the previous   15._____

16. Due to rational ignorance (a) voters choose to ignore political issues and vote along party lines (b) voters protest at the polls (c) voters do not investigate the costs and benefits of elected officials' proposals (d) voters do not understand the issues   16._____

17. Sin taxes would most likely be applied to (a) milk (b) beef (c) cigarettes (d) vacations   17._____

18. Which of the following is an example of a benefits-received principle tax? (a) a sales tax on books (b) a fee charged to see the Grand Canyon (c) an income tax (d) a sales tax on ice cream   18._____

19. Payroll taxes directly support (a) Social Security (b) welfare programs (c) the military (d) Medicaid.   19._____

20. The largest source of local revenue is (a) sales tax (b) state and federal aid (c) user fees (d) property tax   20._____

Part 3—Short Answer

Directions: Read the following questions, and write your response.

21. Define the conditions under which the efficient level of a public good is achieved.

22. Describe a scenario that illustrates the free-rider problem.

Part 4—Critical Thinking

23. How can the marginal tax rate reduce the incentive to work, save, and invest?

24. Why might a state choose not to levy a sales tax on all goods and services?

25. What might be a reason regarding the trend toward more production by the private sector?

Lesson 15.1 Evolution of Fiscal Policy

Part 1—True or False

Directions: Place a *T* for True or an *F* for False in the Answers column to show whether each of the following statements is true or false.

Answers

1. The goal of fiscal policy is to achieve an unemployment rate of zero percent.   1._____

2. The Employment Act of 1946 barred the federal government from promoting full employment and price stability.   2._____

3. Although the economy might exceed its potential output in the short run, it cannot exceed its potential in the long run.   3._____

4. There is no cyclical employment at the natural rate of unemployment.   4._____

5. A contractionary gap results when the economy is exceeding its potential output.   5._____

6. Before the 1930s, fiscal policy was seldom used to influence the overall performance of the economy.   6._____

7. Keynes believed that fiscal policy could only be used in times of low unemployment for it to be effective.   7._____

8. The multiplier effect says that changes in fiscal policy affect aggregate demand by more than the original change in spending or taxing.   8._____

9. It is beneficial in the long run when the economy exceeds its potential output.   9._____

10. Keynes believed that the economy would automatically return to it potential output in a relatively short period of time.   10._____

Part 2—Multiple Choice

Directions: In the Answers column, write the letter that represents the word, or group of words, that correctly completes the statement or answers the question.

Answers

11. What prompted the creation of Keynesian theory? (a) World War I (b) World War II (c) the Vietnam War (d) the Great Depression   11._____

12. With which of the following statements would a classical economist most likely agree? (a) the source of unemployment lies within the market system (b) natural market forces cannot end a recession (c) the government should not interfere in the marketplace (d) natural market forces alone cannot move an economy toward achieving potential output   12._____

13. Which of the following will result if the economy achieves its potential output? (a) the rate of inflation is very low (b) unemployment slightly increases (c) there is full employment (d) the rate of inflation drops rapidly   13._____

14. What will most likely result if output exceeds the economy's potential? (a) higher inflation rate (b) unemployment that exceeds its natural rate (c) the government reduces taxes (d) the government increases its spending   14._____

15. Which of the following is the current estimate of the natural rate of unemployment? (a) 0 percent (b) 4 percent (c) 1 percent (d) 10 percent   15._____

---

16. With which of the following statements would John Maynard Keynes most likely agree?   16._____
    (a) Prices and wages are flexible in the long run. (b) Business expectations can discourage
    firms from investing. (c) Changes in government spending have little effect on aggregate
    demand. (d) Market forces can return the economy to full employment quickly.

17. Suppose that during a major war, a country exceeds its potential output. What will most likely   17._____
    happen in the long run after the war is over? (a) unemployment will increase (b) the country
    will once again perform at its potential output (c) inflation rates will decline (d) all of the
    previous

18. Which of the following best defines the multiplier effect of fiscal policy? (a) A change in   18._____
    fiscal policy affects aggregate demand by more than the original change in spending or
    taxing. (b) A change in fiscal policy affects aggregate demand by less than the original
    change in spending or taxing. (c) A change in fiscal policy affects aggregate demand by the
    same amount as the original change in spending or taxing. (d) A change in fiscal policy does
    not affect aggregate demand in any way.

19. What did maintaining an annually balanced budget usually cause? (a) decreased   19._____
    unemployment during recessions (b) overheated economy during expansions (c) increased
    unemployment during recessions (d) both b and c are correct

20. An expansionary gap would result from which of the following situations? (a) the economy   20._____
    is performing at its potential output (b) the economy is not producing as much as it can
    (c) output exceeds the economy's potential (d) none of the previous

Part 3—Short Answer

Directions: Read the following questions, and write your response.

21. What does a contractionary gap indicate about output in the short run?

22. What does an expansionary gap indicate about output in the short run?

23. What happens in the long run if production exceeds the economy's output potential?

24. Which economist originated the idea of laissez-faire?

Part 4—Critical Thinking

Directions: Read the following questions, and write your response.

25. How did classical economists propose to balance the budget?

26. Explain Keynes's theory of "sticky" prices and wages.

Lesson **15.2** Fiscal Policy Reconsidered

Part 1—True or False

Directions: Place a *T* for True or an *F* for False in the Answers column to show whether each of the following statements is true or false.

Answers

1. Automatic stabilizers boost aggregate demand during periods of recession.   1._____

2. It is impossible to fight unemployment and inflation at the same time with fiscal policy in the short run.   2._____

3. The natural rate of unemployment should be estimated before any discretionary fiscal policies are adopted.   3._____

4. Discretionary fiscal policy is an effective way to end stagflation in the short run.   4._____

5. Fiscal policy can sometimes affect aggregate supply unintentionally.   5._____

6. Lags make it easier to carry out discretionary fiscal policy.   6._____

7. Automatic stabilizers completely eliminate economic fluctuations.   7._____

8. Automatic stabilizers may affect personal incentives to work, spend, save, and invest.   8._____

9. The economy is less stable today than it was before the onset of the Great Depression.   9._____

10. A typical recession will be more than half over before it is officially recognized.   10._____

Part 2—Multiple Choice

Directions: In the Answers column, write the letter that represents the word, or group of words, that correctly completes the statement or answers the question.

Answers

11. What does stagflation cause? (a) an increase in unemployment (b) a leftward shift of the aggregate supply curve (c) an increase in inflation (d) all of the previous   11._____

12. How much time does it usually take for discretionary fiscal policy to become effective? (a) between 6 and 9 months (b) between 9 and 18 months (c) between 18 and 24 months (d) between 24 and 30 months   12._____

13. In which of the following order do the four lags usually occur? (a) recognition lag, implementation lag, decision-making lag, effectiveness lag (b) recognition lag, decision-making lag, implementation lag, effectiveness lag (c) decision-making lag, implementation lag, recognition lag, effectiveness lag (d) decision-making lag, effectiveness lag, implementation lag, recognition lag   13._____

14. Which of the following is an example of discretionary fiscal policy? (a) Congress votes to increase the amount of unemployment insurance a person may receive. (b) During an economic expansion, income taxes claim a growing percentage of income. (c) The progressive income tax protects against declines in disposable income. (d) The amount of people collecting unemployment insurance increases during a recession.   14._____

15. During which decade was stagflation a major problem? (a) 1920s (b) 1950s (c) 1970s (d) 1990s   15._____

16. Which term applies to the delay that results from time needed to identify a macroeconomic problem? (a) recognition lag (b) effectiveness lag (c) implementation lag (d) decision-making lag

16._____

17. Which of the following is true about automatic stabilizers? (a) They almost always cause the income tax rate to increase. (b) Their goal is to decrease aggregate demand during a recession. (c) They adjust to the ups and downs of the economy to keep disposable income constant. (d) They affect government spending, but not government taxing.

17._____

18. What do automatic stabilizers aim to stabilize? (a) disposable income and aggregate demand (b) unemployment insurance (c) income tax (d) Medicare benefits

18._____

19. What is a drawback of discretionary fiscal policy? (a) It always ends up fueling inflation. (b) Long, unpredictable lags can cause the policy to do more harm than good. (c) It benefits only the wealthiest 10 percent of the population. (d) all of the previous

19._____

20. Which of the following is an example of an automatic stabilizer? (a) unemployment insurance (b) federal income tax (c) progressive income tax (d) all of the previous

20._____

Part 3—Short Answer

Directions: Read the following questions, and write your response.

21. What ended the belief that fiscal policy was the "miracle drug" to cure the economy?

22. How do automatic stabilizers help the economy?

23. What is the double trouble of stagflation?

24. Why are problems with lags inevitable with discretionary fiscal policies?

Part 4—Critical Thinking

Directions: Read the following questions, and write your response.

25. The Gramm-Rudman-Hollings Act of 1985 and the Budget Enforcement Act of 1990 were implemented to control discretionary spending. Do these Acts appear to be effective in the current economy?

26. Why was fiscal policy no match for the challenges of stagflation?

Lesson 15.3 Federal Deficits and Federal Debt

Part 1—True or False

Directions: Place a *T* for True or an *F* for False in the Answers column to show whether each of the following statements is true or false.

Answers

1. Usual measures of the federal debt capture all future liabilities.   1. _____

2. Before the Great Depression, federal surpluses occurred during war years.   2. _____

3. Starting in 2001, automatic stabilizers reduced federal revenues and increased federal   3. _____
   spending as the economy worsened.

4. A budget deficit results when government spending exceeds government revenue.   4. _____

5. Decreased investment spending reduces the effectiveness of federal deficits that are intended 5. _____
   to stimulate aggregate demand.

6. Nearly half the debt is refinanced every year by the government.   6. _____

7. Federal debt adds up all federal deficits and subtracts federal surpluses.   7. _____

8. Investment does not fluctuate as much as GDP does.   8. _____

9. One way to measure debt over time is relative to GDP.   9. _____

Part 2—Multiple Choice

Directions: In the Answers column, write the letter that represents the word, or group of words, that correctly completes the statement or answers the questions.

Answers

10. What is federal debt? (a) the total amount owed by the federal government (b) the amount by   10. _____
    which annual spending exceeds annual revenue (c) the total amount the government owes to
    foreign countries (d) none of the previous

11. When bonds mature, how does the federal government pay off maturing bondholders? (a) by   11. _____
    using the money from an increase in taxes (b) by selling more bonds (c) by borrowing money
    from foreign countries (d) all of the previous

12. How does the federal government finance a budget deficit? (a) by raising income taxes (b) by   12. _____
    cutting funding for specific programs (c) by selling U.S. government securities (d) by
    soliciting for donations

13. How does gross debt differ from debt held by the public? (a) Debt held by the public usually   13. _____
    is higher than gross debt. (b) Gross debt includes debt held by households, firms, non-profit
    institutions, and foreign entities. (c) Gross debt includes U.S. Treasury securities purchased
    by various federal agencies. (d) Economists ignore debt held by the public.

14. Which of the following is a result of crowding out? (a) interest rates decrease (b) private   14. _____
    investment decreases (c) income tax increases (d) aggregate demand increases

15. What percent of the time has the federal budged been in deficit since the Great Depression?   15. _____
    (a) 10 percent (b) 33 percent (c) 50 percent (d) 85 percent

16. Which of the following beliefs is most widely accepted? (a) Debt is not a burden on future
generations because they receive debt service payments. (b) Debt becomes more of a burden
on future generations because as foreigners buy more bonds, future debt service payments no
longer remain in the country. (c) Debt is a burden on future generations because one
generation is passing on to the next generation the burden of its borrowing. (d) None of the
above are considered to be widely accepted.

16._____

17. How is *crowding in* defined? (a) Private investment increases when higher government
deficits drive up interest rates. (b) Private investment falls when higher government deficits
drive up interest rates. (c) Government borrowing and spending stimulates private investment
in an otherwise dead economy. (d) A decrease in spending stimulates private investment.

17._____

18. During what year did the United States experience a budget surplus? (a) 1945 (b) 1972
(c) 2000 (d) the United States has never experienced a budget surplus

18._____

19. What is the most likely reason why the federal budget has been in deficit for such a long
period of time? (a) Public officials try to maximize their political support by spending more
than they tax. (b) It is impossible to balance a budget of this size. (c) Since the budget has
been in deficit every single year since the Great Depression, government officials have given
up on trying to achieve a balanced budget. (d) all of the previous

19._____

Part 3—Short Answer

Directions: Read the following questions, and write your response.

20. What is the relationship between budget deficits and the national debt?

21. How does the federal government finance a deficit?

22. What accounted for the budget surpluses of the late 1990s?

Part 4—Critical Thinking

Directions: Read the following questions, and write your response.

23. Keynes made light of people's concerns over increasing deficits with the comment, "In the long run, we're
all dead." Should we be concerned about an increasing national debt?

24. What does the crowding out effect have to do with interest rates?

25. Consider the graph in Figure 15.6 of federal debt as a percentage of GDP. Make and support a prediction
for the graph through the year 2020.

Chapter ⬤15 Review

Part 1—True or False

Directions: Place a *T* for True or an *F* for False in the Answers column to show whether each of the following statements is true or false.

Answers

1. Stagflation can be caused by a leftward shift of the aggregate supply curve.   1._____

2. The federal government finances a budget deficit by selling government securities.   2._____

3. Higher inflation most likely will result if output exceeds the economy's potential.   3._____

4. Since the Great Depression, the federal budget has been in deficit in every year.   4._____

5. Aggregate demand increases as a result of crowding out.   5._____

6. The natural rate of unemployment is zero percent.   6._____

7. Stagflation was a major problem in the 1970s.   7._____

8. Before the 1930s, fiscal policy was often used to influence the overall performance of the   8._____
   economy.

9. A budget deficit results when government spending exceeds government revenue.   9._____

10. Automatic stabilizers aim to decrease aggregate demand during a recession.   10._____

Part 2—Multiple Choice

Directions: In the Answers column, write the letter that represents the word, or group of words, that correctly completes the statement or answers the question.

Answers

11. Which of the following is an example of discretionary fiscal policy? (a) The progressive   11._____
    income tax protects against declines in disposable income. (b) Congress votes to increase the
    income tax for the wealthiest 10 percent of the nation. (c) The amount of people collecting
    unemployment insurance decreases during an expansion. (d) A war causes the economy to
    exceed its potential output.

12. If output exceeds the economy's potential, then (a) the government will increase its spending   12._____
    (b) there will be lower inflation (c) there will be higher inflation (d) unemployment will
    exceed its natural rate.

13. Which of the following is true about stagflation? (a) Stagflation is caused by an economy that   13._____
    exceeds its potential. (b) Stagflation is caused by government deficit spending. (c) Stagflation
    is caused by a shortage in the money supply. (d) Stagflation is caused by a shift in the
    aggregate supply curve.

14. Automatic stabilizers (a) are intended to keep disposable income and spending constant   14._____
    (b) do not affect government taxing (c) always cause the income tax rate to increase (d) all
    of the previous

15. Which of the following best defines the multiplier effect of fiscal policy? (a) a contractionary 15._____
    gap results when the economy is exceeding its potential output (b) a change in fiscal policy
    affects aggregate demand by more than the original change in spending or taxing (c) the
    amount by which annual spending exceeds annual revenue (d) none of the previous

16. If output is below the economy's potential, policy makers often decide to (a) increase taxes or reduce government spending (b) reduce taxes and government spending (c) reduce taxes or increase government spending (d) increase taxes and government spending.   16._____

17. How much time does it usually take for discretionary fiscal policy to become effective? (a) between 1 and 3 months (b) between 3 and 6 months (c) between 6 and 9 months (d) between 9 and 18 months.   17._____

18. Gross debt (a) is usually less than debt held by the public (b) includes debt held by households and firms (c) includes U.S. Treasury securities purchased by various federal agencies (d) includes all the debt in the public and private sphere   18._____

19. Which type of lag usually occurs first? (a) recognition lag (b) implementation lag (c) decision-making lag (d) effectiveness lag.   19._____

20. Crowding in is defined as (a) the ability of government deficits to reduce private investment (b) the ability of government deficits to stimulate private investment (c) the ability of government deficits to drive up interest rates (d) none of the previous.   20._____

Part 3—Short Answer

Directions: Read the following questions, and write your response.

21. How is it possible for output to exceed the economy's potential? Why is this undesirable?

22. Identify and define the two tools of fiscal policy and their effects on the economy.

Part 4—Critical Thinking

Directions: Read the following questions, and write your response.

23. How was fiscal policy used to reduce the effects of the Great Depression?

24. Provide an example of how knowledge of economic history can assist policy makers today in avoiding negative secondary effects of discretionary fiscal policies?

25. What might be a reason for increased ownership of debt by foreigners?

Lesson 16.1 Origins of Money

Part 1—True or False

Directions: Place a *T* for True or an *F* for False in the Answers column to show whether each of the following statements is true or false.

Answers

1. A unit of account is defined as a standard on which to base prices.　　　　　　　1._____

2. The ideal money should have an unlimited supply.　　　　　　　　　　　　　2._____

3. The introduction of commodity money increased the transaction costs of exchange compared with barter.　　3._____

4. Money is anything that is widely accepted in exchange for goods and services.　　4._____

5. Erratic fluctuations in the supply or demand of money increase its usefulness.　　5._____

6. Money, in some kind of form, has existed for as long as humans have.　　　　　6._____

7. The specialization of labor resulted in exchange.　　　　　　　　　　　　　7._____

8. The earliest known coins appeared in the 1700s.　　　　　　　　　　　　　8._____

9. Paper money is a greater source of seigniorage than is coin money.　　　　　　9._____

10. Money is a stock measure and income is a flow measure.　　　　　　　　　　10._____

Part 2—Multiple Choice

Directions: In the Answers column, write the letter that represents the word, or group of words, that correctly completes the statement or answers the question.

Answers

11. Which of the following is true about the barter system? (a) As people began specializing in more goods, the barter system became even more convenient. (b) A huge difference in the values of the units to be exchanged made barter increasingly easy. (c) Greater specialization increased the transaction costs of barter. (d) all of the previous are true　　11._____

12. Which of the following is an example of commodity money? (a) salt (b) corn (c) gold (d) all of the previous　　12._____

13. Which of the following would come closest to the ideal money? (a) bars of gold (b) leaves of paper (c) grains of rice (d) precious stones　　13._____

14. If a person earns seigniorage, what is he or she really earning? (a) the revenue earned from coinage (b) exclusive rights to produce money (c) the power over how much money is in circulation (d) all of the previous　　14._____

15. Why were silver and gold coined? (a) so amounts could more easily be determined (b) to make it easier to carry (c) so the quality of the metals could more easily be determined (d) all of the previous　　15._____

16. What originally prompted money to emerge? (a) Carrying goods around for the sake of bartering became tiresome. (b) The high transaction costs of bartering made people look for an alternative. (c) Goods and services became too specialized. (d) Those in power demanded that the barter system be dropped.　　16._____

17. Which of the following was actually used as money in the past? (a) cattle (b) shells (c) salt   17._____
(d) all of the previous

18. Which of the following characteristics does ideal money have? (a) indivisible (b) high   18._____
opportunity cost (c) of uniform quality (d) supply fluctuates rather erratically

19. Which of the following is true about token money? (a) Its exchange value exceeds the cost of   19._____
production. (b) Its production increases the U.S. government's debt. (c) It is not uniform in
quality. (d) It has a high opportunity cost.

20. Which of the following is **not** considered to be a function of money? (a) unit of account   20._____
(b) an indicator of power (c) a medium of exchange (c) a store of value

Part 3—Short Answer

Directions: Read the following questions, and write your response.

21. Why is money considered to be a stock measure?

22. How did coinage solve the quality-control problem of gold and silver?

23. How are coins and paper money a source of seigniorage for the federal government?

Part 4—Critical Thinking

24. **Directions:** State the advantages (A) or limitations (L) of using human hair as commodity money. How
does it meet or not meet the seven ideals?

Durable	
Portable	
Divisible	
Uniform quality	
Low opportunity cost	
Supply and demand must not fluctuate	
Limited supply	

Lesson 16.2 Origins of Banking and the Federal Reserve System

Part 1—True or False

Directions: Place a *T* for True or an *F* for False in the Answers column to show whether each of the following statements is true or false.

Answers

1. Mutual savings banks account for most thrift institutions.   1._____

2. A well-regulated system of fiat money is more efficient than commodity money or   2._____
   representative money.

3. All national banks became members of the Federal Reserve System when it was created and   3._____
   were subject to new regulations.

4. Early checks could be redeemed for gold by anyone presenting them to the issuing bank.   4._____

5. Commercial banks are the oldest government-chartered depository institutions in the United   5._____
   States.

6. The power of the Federal Reserve System is vested in each of the 12 Reserve Banks.   6._____

7. Open-market operations consist of buying or selling U.S. government securities to influence   7._____
   the money supply and interest rates.

8. Fiat money is redeemable for things of intrinsic value.   8._____

9. Historically, savings and loan associations specialized in home mortgage loans.   9._____

10. Commercial banks are the only depository institutions that offer demand deposits.   10._____

Part 2—Multiple Choice

Directions: In the Answers column, write the letter that represents the word, or group of words, that correctly completes the statement or answers the question.

Answers

11. What do credit unions do? (a) extend loans to members to finance homes or other major   11._____
    consumer purchases (b) lend money for commercial ventures (c) offer demand deposits to
    anyone (d) none of the previous

12. Which of the following is an example of representative money? (a) gold coins (b) bank notes   12._____
    that could be traded for gold (c) paper dollar bills (d) gold bars

13. Which of the following is an example of a thrift institution? (a) commercial banks (b) demand   13._____
    deposit banks (c) mutual savings banks (d) all of the previous

14. Why is fiat money more desirable than commodity money? (a) because it has intrinsic value   14._____
    (b) because it does not tie up valuable resources (c) because not many people accept it as
    money (d) all of the previous

15. Which of the following best defines the fractional reserve banking system? (a) bank notes are   15._____
    exchanged for a specific commodity (b) depositors' money is insured (c) only a portion of
    bank deposits are backed by reserves (d) none of the previous

16. If a bank has reserves valued at $500 but deposits totaling $1,000, what is the reserve ratio? 16._____
    (a) 10 percent (b) 30 percent (c) 50 percent (d) 200 percent

17. Which of the following is true about most depository institutions? (a) They make loans from   17.____
   their deposits. (b) They may be commercial banks or thrift institutions. (c) They accept
   deposits from the public. (d) all of the previous

18. The United States' dual banking system allows for the existence of which two institutions?   18.____
   (a) commercial banks and open-market operations (b) state banks and national banks
   (c) the fractional reserve banking system and the Fed (d) state banks and commercial banks

19. What did the Federal Reserve System do when it came into power? (a) took away national   19.____
   banks' power to issue bank notes and gave it to the Federal Reserve Banks (b) began dealing
   with the public directly (c) required that state banks joined it (d) all of the previous

Part 3—Short Answer

Directions: Read the following questions, and write your response.

20. How did bank checks reduce transaction costs among traders?

21. Why must banks keep a reserve ratio on hand?

22. What differentiates commercial banks from thrifts?

23. Which banking system has the power to issue bank notes, and who actually prints the bank notes?

24. What is the most important tool of monetary policy, and what does it affect?

Part 4—Critical Thinking

Directions: Read the following questions, and write your response.

25. What might be required in an economy for a smooth transition from representative money to fiat money?

26. Why does a dual banking system exist in the United States?

27. How is the Board of Governors of the Federal Reserve System protected from political party influences?

Lesson **16.3** Money, Near Money, and Credit Cards

Part 1—True or False

Directions: Place a *T* for True or an *F* for False in the Answers column to show whether each of the following statements is true or false.

Answers

1. The definition of money does not include credit cards.   1. _____

2. Funds deposited in money market mutual fund accounts are used to purchase short-term   2. _____
   interest-earning assets by the financial institution that administers the fund.

3. M3 is more liquid than M2.   3. _____

4. The money supply at any given time is a stock measure.   4. _____

5. Demand deposits are held mostly by commercial banks and generally earn no interest.   5. _____

6. Federal Reserve notes are fiat money.   6. _____

7. The only difference between M1 and M2 is that M2 also consists of savings deposits.   7. _____

8. Currency makes up almost all of M1.   8. _____

9. More than half of all Federal Reserve notes are in foreign countries.   9. _____

10. U.S. coins are token money.   10. _____

Part 2—Multiple Choice

Directions: In the Answers column, write the letter that represents the word, or group of words, that correctly completes the statement or answers the questions.

Answers

11. Of the various definitions of money, which is the largest? (a) M1 (b) M2 (c) M3 (d) It cannot   11. _____
    be determined from the information given.

12. Which of the following makes up about half of M1, as compared to the others? (a) traveler's   12. _____
    checks (b) currency (c) demand deposits (d) It cannot be determined from the information
    given.

13. What are holders of time deposits issued? (a) bank notes (b) CDs (c) credit cards (d) checks   13. _____

14. Which of the following is true of savings deposits? (a) They have a specific maturity date.   14. _____
    (b) Withdrawals are penalized. (c) They earn interest. (d) They serve as a direct medium of
    exchange.

15. What does M1 include? (a) currency held by the nonbanking public (b) money in bank vaults   15. _____
    (c) savings deposits (d) all of the previous

16. Which of the following progressions is most accurate? (a) paper money → commodity money   16. _____
    → electronic entry (b) fiat money → commodity money → electronic entry (c) fiat money →
    electronic entry → paper money (d) commodity money → paper money → electronic entry

17. Which of the following is **not** an example of a small-denomination time deposit? (a) $50   17. _____
    (b) $27,000 (c) $110,000 (d) $1,000

18. Which of the following is true of money market mutual fund accounts? (a) An unlimited   18. _____
    number of checks can be written per month. (b) There are restrictions on the minimum
    balance. (c) Checks can be written for any amount. (d) They are a component of M1.

19. Why are traveler's checks safer than cash? (a) Unlike cash, they do not hold intrinsic value.   19. _____
    (b) Travelers are limited to how many traveler's checks they may carry. (c) They can be
    replaced easily. (d) They cannot be counterfeited.

Part 3—Short Answer

Directions: Read the following questions, and write your response.

20. Which measure of money serves as a medium of exchange?

21. How do time deposits differ from savings deposits?

22. What are some of the limitations of money market mutual fund accounts?

23. How is a debit card similar to money?

Part 4—Critical Thinking

Directions: Read the following questions, and write your response.

24. Credit cards are often named as a primary reason for personal financial problems sometimes leading to
    bankruptcy. What makes credit card mismanagement common?

25. Will replacing the use of currency with electronic money in the economy help or hurt personal financial
    management? Why?

Chapter ⬤16 Review

Part 1—True or False

Directions: Place a *T* for True or an *F* for False in the Answers column to show whether each of the following statements is true or false.

Answers

1. The ideal money should have a limited supply.   1._____

2. A well-regulated system of fiat money is more efficient than commodity money or representative money.   2._____

3. Seigniorage is defined as the revenue earned from coinage.   3._____

4. Savings deposits earn interest and have a specific maturity date.   4._____

5. The United States' dual banking system refers to the existence of state banks and commercial banks.   5._____

6. Over the years as people began specializing in producing more goods, the barter system became less desirable.   6._____

7. Money market mutual fund accounts are a component of M1.   7._____

8. Credit unions lend money for commercial ventures.   8._____

9. Paper money in circulation in the United States is representative money.   9._____

10. Farmers served as the first banks.   10._____

Part 2—Multiple Choice

Directions: In the Answers column, write the letter that represents the word, or group of words, that correctly completes the statement or answers the question.

Answers

11. The concept of money emerged because (a) it eased the process of trading between countries (b) it was introduced by the English king (c) the high transaction costs of bartering made people look for an alternative (d) none of the previous.   11._____

12. The broadest definition of money is (a) M1 (b) M2 (c) M3 (d) M4.   12._____

13. The Fed and the U.S. Treasury have announced plans to redesign the currency to (a) combat counterfeiters (b) encourage coin collecting (c) save money (d) all of the previous.   13._____

14. Which of the following is an example of commodity money? (a) cattle (b) gold (c) salt (d) all of the previous.   14._____

15. When you put your earnings into a savings account, you are using money as (a) a medium of exchange (b) a store of value (c) a measure of value (d) a unit of account.   15._____

16. Ideal money (a) is of uniform quality (b) must be a precious metal (c) fluctuates in supply (d) is unlimited in supply   16._____

17. The Federal Reserve System (a) strengthened the power of national banks (b) gave Federal Reserve Banks the power to issue bank notes (c) took over leadership responsibilities for all banks (d) weakened the power of Federal Reserve Banks.   17._____

18. Large-denomination deposits are defined as any deposit more than (a) $50,000 (b) $75,000   18._____
    (c) $100,000 (d) $250,000

19. M1 includes (a) currency held by the nonbanking public (b) currency held by banks (c) money   19._____
    market accounts d) time deposits

20. If a bank has reserves valued at $300 but deposits totaling $1,500, what is the reserve ratio?   20._____
    (a) 3 percent (b) 50 percent (c) 95 percent (d) 20 percent

Part 3—Short Answer

Directions: Read the following questions, and write your response.

21. Identify the three functions of money. Which function is most useful to you in your life right now?

22. What is the narrowest definition of money and what does it include? Which, if any, of the elements do you
    currently possess?

23. What is the discount rate, and why is it not available to the general public?

Part 4—Critical Thinking

24. **Directions:** The following table lists amounts of money held in a variety of ways in August of 1999. Use
    these values to calculate the amount in M1 and M2 at that time.

Money Held in August of 1999 Values in Billions of Dollars	
Currency	$ 302.00
Traveler's Checks	5.20
Checkable Deposits	480.30
Savings Deposits	1,842.50
Small Time Deposits	700.60
Money Market Funds	627.40
M1 =	
M2 =	

Lesson ⬤ 17.1 How Banks Work

Part 1—True or False

Directions: Place a *T* for True or an *F* for False in the Answers column to show whether each of the following statements is true or false.

Answers

1. As long as excess reserves end up as checkable deposits in the banking system, the money multiplier can operate.   1._____

2. The Fed increases the money supply by selling bonds.   2._____

3. The two sides of a balance sheet must always be equal.   3._____

4. The higher the reserve requirement, the larger the money multiplier.   4._____

5. The banking system eliminates excess reserves by expanding the money supply.   5._____

6. Required reserves are not considered to be in the money supply circulation.   6._____

7. Excess reserves fuel the expansion of checkable deposits.   7._____

8. Some banks are not subject to the Fed's reserve requirement.   8._____

9. An individual bank can lend more than its excess reserves.   9._____

10. When the reserve ratio is increased banks are able to increase their lending.   10._____

Part 2—Multiple Choice

Directions: In the Answers column, write the letter that represents the word, or group of words, that correctly completes the statement or answers the question.

Answers

11. Where may a bank store its required reserves? (a) anywhere (b) in the accounts of the banks' customers (c) at the Fed (d) at another nearby bank   11._____

12. If the required reserve ratio is 15 percent, what is the money multiplier? (a) 0.067 (b) 1.0 (c) 6.67 (d) 15   12._____

13. Using the information in item 12 and allowing for rounding, what is the maximum possible change in checkable deposits if the change in excess reserves is $15,000? (a) $100 (b) $1,000 (c) $15,000 (d) $100,000   13._____

14. A bank must go through a variety of steps before it may begin operating. Which of the following choices correctly lists these steps in the order in which they must be completed? (a) incorporate, create a charter, establish assets, establish owners' equity (b) create a charter, establish assets, establish owners' equity, incorporate (c) create a charter, incorporate, establish owners' equity, establish assets (d) establish assets, establish owners' equity, create a charter, incorporate   14._____

15. How does the banking system eliminate excess reserves? (a) by buying up the excess reserves (b) by expanding the money supply (c) by constantly increasing required reserves (d) all of the previous   15._____

16. What is the key to adjusting the multiple expansion of checkable deposits? (a) the fractional reserve system (b) interest rates (c) the required reserve ratio (d) the balance sheet   16._____

17. Which of the following terms is best defined as any physical property or financial claim that is   17._____
    owned? (a) liability (b) net worth (c) excess reserves (d) asset

18. For a given required reserve ratio, when is the multiplier the greatest? (a) when the public does   18._____
    not choose to hold some of the newly created money as cash (b) when borrowed funds sit idle
    in checking accounts (c) when banks allow excess reserves to sit idle (d) all of the previous

19. If a balance sheet indicates that liabilities and net worth equal $1,000,000 and $3,000,000,   19._____
    respectively, what would the assets equal? (a) $1,000,000 (b) $3,000,000 (c) $4,000,000 (d) It
    cannot be determined from the information given.

20. A bank makes money by (a) using its excess reserves to make loans (b) taking money from   20._____
    customers' accounts (c) selling its excess reserves to other banks (d) paying interest to
    depositors

Part 3—Short Answer

Directions: Read the following questions, and write your response.

21. What is the first step in starting up a state bank?

22. What does owners' equity represent for a bank?

23. Like any business, a bank must keep a balance sheet that shows a balance between which two accounts?

24. How does the Fed pay for a U.S. government bond it purchases from a bank?

25. The money multiplier is inversely related to ___?___ .

Part 4—Critical Thinking

Directions: Read the following questions, and write your response.

26. How would an increase in the reserve ratio affect a bank?

27. Explain the saying on the plaque in the Federal Reserve chairman's office, "The buck starts here."

28. How does the Fed reduce the money supply?

Lesson ⬤17.2 Monetary Policy in the Short Run

Part 1—True or False

Directions: Place a *T* for True or an *F* for False in the Answers column to show whether each of the following statements is true or false.

Answers

1. For a given money demand curve, an increase in money supply pushes down the market interest rate.

1. _____

2. A lower interest rate increases real GDP in the short run.

2. _____

3. Banks are unable to lend one another money for short periods of time.

3. _____

4. Money and income are identical.

4. _____

5. Lowering the reserve ratio to create excess reserves reduces the money supply.

5. _____

6. Banks usually try to keep excess reserves to a minimum.

6. _____

7. The federal funds rate is considered to be the Fed's target interest rate.

7. _____

8. Your demand for money is based on your expected spending.

8. _____

9. The big advantage of money is its general acceptance in market exchange.

9. _____

10. The federal funds rate remains constant.

10. _____

Part 2—Multiple Choice

Directions: In the Answers column, write the letter that represents the word, or group of words, that correctly completes the statement or answers the question.

Answers

11. Suppose the Fed reduces discount rates. How would this affect the money supply curve? (a) shift leftward (b) shift rightward (c) movement upward along the curve (d) no effect on the curve

11. _____

12. Who primarily determines the money supply? (a) the Fed (b) the general population (c) banks (d) the president

12. _____

13. The money demand curve is which of the following shapes? (a) downward slope (b) upward slope (c) horizontal line (d) vertical line

13. _____

14. Which of the following is **not** a valid way through which the Fed can reduce the money supply? (a) by selling U.S. government securities (b) by increasing income tax (c) by increasing the discount rate (d) by raising the required reserve ratio

14. _____

15. What is the major drawback of money as compared to other financial assets? (a) not liquid (b) more difficult to come by (c) does not earn interest (d) more difficult to use as a medium of exchange

15. _____

16. What is the federal funds rate? (a) the interest rate charged to corporations (b) the interest rate consumers are charged (c) the interest rate charged when one bank lends money to another bank (d) none of the previous

16. _____

Part 3—Short Answer

Directions: Read the following questions, and write your response.

17. How does the federal funds rate impact the economy?

18. What is a drawback of money as a currency asset?

19. How do increases and decreases in the money supply affect the interest rate?

Part 4—Critical Thinking

Directions: Read the following questions, and write your response.

20. How does the federal funds rate affect other interest rates such as mortgage rates, credit card rates, and interest on CDs?

21. What is the opportunity cost of holding money in the form of currency, demand deposits, and traveler's checks?

Part 5—Graphing

22. **Directions:** Graph the effects of an increased interest rate on aggregate demand. How will this affect the aggregate demand curve?

Lesson 17.3 Monetary Policy in the Long Run

Part 1—True or False

Directions: Place a *T* for True or an *F* for False in the Answers column to show whether each of the following statements is true or false.

Answers

1. Economic stimulation in the short run always leads to a more desirable result in the long run.   1. _____

2. The economy cannot produce more than its potential output in the long run.   2. _____

3. Hyperinflation became a problem for some countries beginning in the eighteenth century.   3. _____

4. An increasing number of central banks around the world are becoming more dependent upon political pressure.   4. _____

5. The effects of deflation are not as severe as those caused by inflation.   5. _____

6. An increase in the money supply doesn't change the economy's potential output.   6. _____

7. Elected officials usually urge the Fed to stimulate the economy whenever it's performing below its potential.   7. _____

8. Each bout of inflation in the United States was preceded by a decrease in the money supply.   8. _____

9. The Fed does not earn a profit.   9. _____

10. The Fed pays no interest on Federal Reserve notes.   10. _____

Part 2—Multiple Choice

Directions: In the Answers column, write the letter that represents the word, or group of words, that correctly completes the statement or answers the questions.

Answers

11. What is the euro? (a) the new common currency for the world (b) essentially, it is the dollar (c) the new common currency for many nations in Europe (d) none of the previous   11. _____

12. Which of the following countries experienced the most drastic hyperinflation during the twentieth century? (a) Germany (b) the United States (c) France (d) Poland   12. _____

13. Which type of lag is usually less severe for monetary policy and more severe for fiscal policy? (a) effectiveness lag (b) recognition lag (c) decision-making lag (d) all of the previous   13. _____

14. What has research led economists to conclude about inflation and how it is affected by political pressure on a central bank? (a) The greater the political pressure on a central bank, the higher the inflation. (b) The greater the political pressure on a central bank, the lower the inflation. (c) The lower the political pressure on a central bank, the higher the inflation. (d) There is no clear relationship between the two.   14. _____

15. What can result from large increases in the money supply in the long run? (a) increase in GDP (b) inflation (c) increase in aggregate demand (d) increase in potential output   15. _____

16. How are money growth and inflation related? (a) inverse relationship (b) direct relationship (c) no relationship (d) none of the previous   16. _____

17. What helps to determine potential output? (a) the state of technology (b) the rules of the game that nurture production and exchange (c) the supply of resources in the economy (d) all of the previous   17. _____

18. The emergence of hyperinflation in any economy is accompanied by (a) a sharp increase in real GDP (b) a decrease of the money supply (c) extremely high interest rates (d) an increase in the supply of money. 18.____

19. Which of the following best describes the shape of the economy's long-run supply curve? (a) an upward-sloping curve (b) a downward-sloping curve (c) a horizontal line (d) a vertical line 19.____

20. What may result from deflation? (a) aggregate demand decreases (b) investment decreases (c) consumers delay major purchases (d) all of the previous 20.____

Part 3—Short Answer

Directions: Read the following questions, and write your response.

21. In the long run, increases in the money supply result in ___?___.

22. The three bouts of high inflation since 1913 were preceded by what economic event?

23. What causes hyperinflation?

24. How does the degree of independence of a central banking system affect the economy's inflation rate?

25. How do the lag times for policy implementation differ for fiscal and monetary policy?

Part 4—Critical Thinking

Directions: Read the following questions, and write your response.

26. How is the Fed like a private, profitable business?

27. Why are falling prices (deflation) an economic problem?

Chapter ⬤17 Review

Part 1—True or False

Directions: Place a *T* for True or an *F* for False in the Answers column to show whether each of the following statements is true or false.

Answers

1. Banks determine the money supply.   1._____

2. The banking system eliminates excess reserves by expanding the money supply.   2._____

3. The greater the political pressure on a central bank, the higher the inflation.   3._____

4. The Fed increases the money supply by selling bonds.   4._____

5. The quantity of money demanded has an inverse relationship to the market interest rate. 5._____

6. Potential output is determined solely by advances in technology.   6._____

7. A bank must first create a charter before it begins operating.   7._____

8. A lower interest rate decreases real GDP in the short run.   8._____

9. Economic stimulation in the short run does not necessarily lead to a more desirable result in the long run.   9._____

10. If the Fed reduces discount rates, the money supply curve would shift to the left.   10._____

Part 2—Multiple Choice

Directions: In the Answers column, write the letter that represents the word, or group of words, that correctly completes the statement or answers the question.

Answers

11. The federal funds rate is (a) the interest rate charged in the government bond market (b) the interest rate charged to the public (c) the interest rate charged by one bank when it loans money to another bank (d) the interest rate charged to corporations.   11._____

12. An asset is defined as (a) the interest rate charged in the federal funds market (b) any physical property or financial claim that is owned (c) bank reserves in excess of required reserves (d) the new European common currency.   12._____

13. Hyperinflation is accompanied by (a) technological improvements (b) an increase in investment (c) political stability (d) an increase in the supply of money.   13._____

14. The money supply curve is which of the following shapes? (a) an upward sloping line (b) a downward sloping line (c) a vertical line (d) a horizontal line   14._____

15. What can result from increases in the money supply in the long run? (a) inflation (b) decrease in unemployment (c) increase in GDP (d) increase in aggregate demand   15._____

16. The Fed can reduce the money supply by (a) increasing income tax (b) raising the required reserves ratio (c) decreasing the discount rate (d) lowering taxes   16._____

17. If the required reserve ratio is 8 percent, what is the money multiplier? (a) 12.5 (b) 1.0 (c) 1.8 (d) 8   17._____

18. If the required reserve ratio is 5 percent, a bank must keep at least how much more on reserve   18.____
when a $500,000 deposit is made? (a) $25,000 (b) $500,000 (c) $5,000 (d) $2,500.

19. A decrease in the money supply will cause the money supply curve to shift __?__ and the   19.____
market interest to __?__. (a) left/fall (b) left/increase (c) right/fall (d) right/increase

20. For a given required reserve ratio, the multiplier is greatest when (a) Borrowed funds sit idle   20.____
in checking accounts. (b) The Fed increases the money supply. (c) The public does not hold
some of the newly created money as cash. (d) The public holds most of the newly created
money as cash.

Part 3—Short Answer

Directions: Read the following questions, and write your response.

21. Suppose the Fed wants to expand the money supply. How might it achieve this? How might this affect
your saving and borrowing?

22. Why is deflation harmful to the economy? What might result?

Part 4—Critical Thinking

23. Suppose you and a few colleagues would like to open a national bank. What steps would you have to take
to do so? After your first day of business, you must fill out the bank's balance sheet. You and your
colleagues have invested $700,000 in cash in the bank and $500,000 on building and furniture. So far the
bank has received a total of $200,000 in deposits but it has made no loans. Fill out the balance sheet below
to reflect this.

Assets		Liabilities and Net Worth	
Cash		Checkable Deposits	
Building and Furniture		Net Worth	
Total		Total	

Lesson   18.1   Benefits of Trade

Part 1—True or False

Directions: Place a *T* for True or an *F* for False in the Answers column to show whether each of the following statements is true or false.

Answers

1. Exports are becoming less and less important for the United States.   1._____

2. Because the United States has an educated labor force and high-tech capital, it experiences greater productivity per worker than many other nations.   2._____

3. Tastes and preferences rarely differ across countries.   3._____

4. Australians import more wine than the French.   4._____

5. Capital goods and industrial supplies make up the majority of U.S. exports.   5._____

6. Seasonal difference may help countries decide which goods to export.   6._____

7. The United States exports more automobiles than it imports.   7._____

8. Countries export what they can produce at a lower opportunity cost.   8._____

9. Taiwan receives a great deal of American exports.   9._____

10. The United States exports coffee.   10._____

Part 2—Multiple Choice

Directions: In the Answers column, write the letter that represents the word, or group of words, that correctly completes the statement or answers the question.

Answers

11. If countries specialize in certain goods, what is the result? (a) unemployment increases (b) real GDP decreases (c) world output increases (d) inflation   11._____

12. Which of the following countries exports the smallest proportion of GDP? (a) Egypt (b) the Netherlands (c) Germany (d) Canada   12._____

13. What is the largest category of U.S. exports? (a) consumer goods (b) capital goods (c) food stuffs (d) none of the previous   13._____

14. Of the following choices, which mineral is most abundant in the United States? (a) coal (b) oil (c) diamonds (d) The United States does not possess any of these minerals.   14._____

15. How do countries decide what to produce? (a) They take the amount of resources they possess into account. (b) They take the quality of resources they possess into account. (c) They take the type of resources they possess into account. (d) all of the previous   15._____

16. How can a country maximize the benefits of trade? (a) by importing all of its goods (b) by exporting all of its goods (c) by specializing in goods it produces with the lowest opportunity costs (d) none of the previous   16._____

17. Exports of goods and services amounted to what percentage of U.S. GDP in 2002? (a) 10 percent (b) 20 percent (c) 30 percent (d) 40 percent   17._____

18. Which of the following countries receives the most goods from the United States? (a) China (b) Canada (c) South Korea (d) France   18._____

19. Which of the following is **not** considered to be a country's resource? (a) labor (b) minerals   19._____
(c) type of government (d) climate

20. Exporting which of the following goods allows the United States to gain the maximum   20._____
benefit from trade? (a) grains (b) bananas (c) coffee (d) all of the previous

Part 3—Short Answer

Directions: Read the following questions, and write your response.

21. What country's comparative advantage has lured the manufacturing industries away from Mexico?

22. Explain what opportunity cost has to do with specialization and trade.

23. How do economies of scale enable countries to gain from specialization and trade?

24. What goods and services does the United States export?

25. What goods and services are imported into the United States?

Part 4—Critical Thinking

Directions: Read the following questions, and write your response.

26. Why are consumption patterns important for world trade? What imported products meet your preferences?

27. What may be some determining factors for a new business to consider selling goods and services overseas
instead of concentrating only on the domestic market?

Name _____ Class _____ Date _____

Lesson 18.2 Trade Restrictions and Free-Trade Agreements

Part 1—True or False

Directions: Place a *T* for True or an *F* for False in the Answers column to show whether each of the following statements is true or false.

Answers

1. Average tariffs are lower now than at any time in history.   1._____
2. Trade rounds have been successful in lowering tariffs.   2._____
3. World output and world trade has decreased since the mid-twentieth century.   3._____
4. Free trade agreements are becoming more popular around the world.   4._____
5. The European Union makes free trade even more difficult.   5._____
6. A quota never targets imports from a particular country.   6._____
7. The world price usually is lower than the U.S. price of a certain good.   7._____
8. The revenue from tariffs goes to the government.   8._____
9. Trade restrictions often cause other countries to adopt their own trade restrictions. 9._____
10. Tariffs were at an all-time low during the Great Depression.   10._____

Part 2—Multiple Choice

Directions: In the Answers column, write the letter that represents the word, or group of words, that correctly completes the statement or answers the question.

Answers

11. Trade restrictions can have which of the following effects? (a) slower economic progress   11._____
    (b) high transaction costs (c) decreased competition (d) all of the previous

12. Who benefits from a quota on imported goods to the United States? (a) the U.S. consumer (b)   12._____
    the U.S. government (c) U.S. producers of the product (d) U.S. exporters

13. What does the World Trade Organization (WTO) do? (a) It serves the exact same role as the   13._____
    General Agreement on Tariffs and Trade (GATT). (b) It controls trade for a given period of
    time. (c) It deals with services and trade-related aspects of intellectual property. (d) all of the
    previous

14. What effect does a tariff on imports to the United States have? (a) the quantity of imports   14._____
    increases (b) the quantity of imports decreases (c) the supply of goods in the U.S. market
    increases (d) the price of goods in the U.S. market decreases

15. Which of the following is **not** a way to restrict free trade? (a) domestic content requirements 15._____
    (b) the banning of tariffs (c) quotas (d) stringent safety standards

16. What did those who supported the General Agreement on Tariffs and Trade (GATT) agree to   16._____
    do? (a) reduce tariffs (b) increase quotas (c) favor some nations over others when trading
    (d) all of the previous

17. Which of the following countries is involved in the North American Free Trade Agreement   17._____
    (NAFTA)? (a) Mexico (b) the United States (c) Canada (d) all of the previous

18. Who benefits from a tariff on U.S. imports? (a) U.S. producers (b) foreign producers (c) U.S.   18._____
consumers (d) all of the previous

19. Which of the following was the first to try to negotiate lower tariffs and quotas? (a) North   19._____
American Free Trade Agreement (NAFTA) (b) the General Agreement on Tariffs and Trade
(GATT) (c) the Uruguay Round (d) the World Trade Organization (WTO)

20. What do quotas do? (a) impose a tax on U.S. imports (b) impose a limit on the quantity of   20._____
imports (c) bar some countries from selling imports to the United States (d) all of the previous

Part 3—Short Answer

Directions: Read the following questions, and write your response.

21. Who do trade restrictions help and who do they harm?

22. How do tariffs reduce the quantity of imports?

23. What is the purpose of apparel quotas in the United States?

24. What is the function of the World Trade Organization?

25. What is the current trend with tariffs worldwide?

Part 4—Critical Thinking

Directions: Read the following questions, and write your response.

26. How do trade restrictions affect global trade?

27. What causes a trade war?

28. What do you believe will be the greatest obstacle to the passage of an FTAA (Free Trade Area of the
Americas)? Do you think this agreement is a good idea? Why or why not?

Lesson 18.3 Balance of Payments

Part 1—True or False

Directions: Place a *T* for True or an *F* for False in the Answers column to show whether each of the following statements is true or false.

Answers

1. The current account balance figure is reported once a year by the federal government. 1._____

2. Some international transactions are impossible to trace. 2._____

3. Since the mid-1970s, imports have exceeded exports every year in the United States. 3._____

4. The balance on goods and services is the value of exports of goods and services minus the value of imports of goods and services. 4._____

5. Goods, but not services, can be traded internationally. 5._____

6. Unilateral transfers include personal gifts to friends and relatives who live abroad. 6._____

7. The balance of payments is a flow measure. 7._____

8. U.S. government grants to foreign governments are not included in calculating net unilateral transfers. 8._____

9. For more years than not, the United States has run a trade surplus. 9._____

10. Applying the statistical discrepancy is considered illegal. 10._____

Part 2—Multiple Choice

Directions: In the Answers column, write the letter that represents the word, or group of words, that correctly completes the statement or answers the question.

Answers

11. Which of the following would the financial account track? (a) an Argentinean company buys 100 acres of land in Utah (b) a grandfather in California buys his grandson, who lives in Connecticut, stock in a company (c) a family from Wisconsin purchases their first home in Texas (d) all of the previous 11._____

12. What must happen to create a trade deficit? (a) The United States is exporting more than it is importing. (b) The value of merchandise imports is greater than the value of merchandise exports. (c) Imports are at an all-time low. (d) all of the previous 12._____

13. If the current account balance is negative, which of the following is true? (a) There is a current account equilibrium. (b) There is a current account surplus. (c) There is a current account deficit. (d) Double-entry bookkeeping has not been used consistently. 13._____

14. Which of the following would be included in the U.S. balance of payments? (a) A Chilean bread company buys grain from the United States. (b) The United States imports electronics from Taiwan. (c) The United States sells coal to Italy. (d) all of the previous 14._____

15. What is one possible disadvantage to having a trade surplus in the United States? (a) American workers are replaced by foreign workers. (b) Americans are buying more foreign assets instead of American-made goods and services. (c) Foreigners compete with U.S. consumers to purchase U.S. made goods. (d) America's productive capacity decreases. 15._____

16. What must result from double-entry bookkeeping? (a) trade surplus (b) total credits equal total debits (c) a positive balance (d) a negative balance 16._____

17. What is the purpose of statistical discrepancy? (a) to measure the error in the balance-of-payments data (b) to create a trade surplus (c) to create a trade deficit (d) to make it appear that the economy is doing better than it actually is   17.____

18. The United States earns money to pay off the current account deficit by (a) buying financial assets (b) buying real assets (c) buying housing and land (d) selling stocks and bonds   18.____

19. Which of the following best defines the term *current accounts*? (a) record of all economic transactions between residents of one country and residents of the rest of the world (b) the value of a country's exported goods minus the value of its imported goods during a given period (c) that portion of the balance of payments that records exports and imports of goods and services, net investment income, and net transfers (d) that portion of the balance of payments that records international transactions involving financial assets and real assets   19.____

20. Which of the following is an example of a U.S. service import? (a) Customer service calls for an American company are answered by workers in India. (b) An Australian takes a vacation in California. (c) The Olympic Games are held in Cincinnati. (d) all of the previous   20.____

Part 3—Short Answer

Directions: Read the following questions, and write your response.

21. How does double-entry book keeping allow the economic transactions between the United States and the rest of the world to balance?

22. Why does the merchandise trade balance not balance?

23. With which country does the United States hold the greatest trade deficit?

24. What are some of the services that are traded internationally?

25. What is the trade status of the U.S. financial account?

Part 5 —Critical Thinking

Directions: Read the following questions, and write your response.

26. Is a growing trade deficit necessarily a problem for the U.S. economy? Why or why not?

27. How do net unilateral transfers affect the current account balance?

Lesson 18.4 Foreign Exchange Rates

Part 1—True or False

Directions: Place a *T* for True or an *F* for False in the Answers column to show whether each of the following statements is true or false.

Answers

1. American residents can pay for most goods and services in the euro area with dollars. 1._____

2. The foreign exchange market never closes. 2._____

3. The cheaper it is to buy euros, the higher the dollar price of euro-area products. 3._____

4. Arbitrageurs take fewer risks than speculators. 4._____

5. People in countries suffering from economic and political turmoil may buy dollars to ensure their financial stability. 5._____

6. When the exchange rate is flexible, government officials usually have little direct role in foreign exchange markets. 6._____

7. Speculators simultaneously buy currency in one market and sell it in another. 7._____

8. Central bank intervention is necessary to ensure a flexible exchange rate. 8._____

9. Currency appreciation occurs for the U.S. dollar when there is an increase in the dollar price of a euro. 9._____

10. One of the factors assumed constant along the demand curve are the incomes and preferences of U.S. consumers. 10._____

Part 2—Multiple Choice

Directions: In the Answers column, write the letter that represents the word, or group of words, that correctly completes the statement or answers the question.

Answers

11. What is the result if the dollar price of a euro increases? (a) flexible exchange rates (b) fixed exchange rates (c) currency depreciation for the U.S. dollar (d) currency appreciation for the U.S. dollar 11._____

12. Why did the value of the dollar begin to float? (a) The U.S. government relaxed its control on the value of the dollar. (b) The value of the dollar was no longer tied to gold. (c) Foreign countries began to use the dollar as their standard currency. (d) none of the previous 12._____

13. What determines the exchange rate? (a) the United States government (b) the governments of foreign countries (c) the interaction of demand and supply for currencies (d) the exchange rate is fixed 13._____

14. Why did European countries create and implement the euro? (a) to make financial interactions less complicated (b) to become more productive (c) to become more competitive with the United States (d) all of the previous 14._____

15. Suppose that there is a decrease in U.S. income. What effect would this have on the U.S. demand curve for euros? (a) shift to the left (b) shift to the right (c) upward movement along the curve (d) downward movement along the curve 15._____

16. Suppose that there is an increase in U.S. income. What effect would this have on the U.S. supply curve for euros? (a) shift to the left (b) shift to the right (c) no effect (d) It would become a vertical line.

16. _____

Part 3—Short Answer

Directions: Read the following questions, and write your response.

17. What determines the currency exchange rate between two countries?

18. What overriding reason causes increased U.S. demand for a particular country's currency?

19. What shows that a foreign currency has appreciated or depreciated?

Part 4—Critical Thinking

Directions: Read the following questions, and write your response.

20. How is a currency speculator like a day trader in the stock market?

21. If a floating exchange rate is ideal, why do some smaller countries choose to fix the value of their currency in terms of dollars?

Part 5—Graphing

22. **Directions**: Graph the effect of a decrease in demand for U.S. dollars worldwide. How will this affect the exchange rate for U.S. dollars relative to euros?

Chapter ⬤18 Review

Part 1—True or False

Directions: Place a *T* for True or an *F* for False in the Answers column to show whether each of the following statements is true or false.

Answers

1. The U.S. consumer benefits more than any other party involved when a quota is imposed. 1._____

2. A trade deficit forms when the United States is exporting more than it is importing. 2._____

3. Imposing stringent safety standards is a way to restrict free trade. 3._____

4. The largest category of U.S. exports is consumer goods. 4._____

5. Countries look to the amount, type, and quality of the resources they possess when determining what to produce. 5._____

6. If a current account balance is negative, then there is a current account deficit. 6._____

7. The World Trade Organization deals with services and trade-related aspects of intellectual property. 7._____

8. The United States obtains money to pay off the current account deficit by selling stocks and bonds. 8._____

9. The United States enjoys one of the highest rates of productivity per worker. 9._____

10. In general, trade rounds have not been successful in lowering tariffs. 10._____

Part 2—Multiple Choice

Directions: In the Answers column, write the letter that represents the word, or group of words, that correctly completes the statement or answers the question.

Answers

11. Which of the following countries is involved in the North American Free Trade Agreement (NAFTA)? (a) Thailand (b) Mexico (c) Korea (d) Egypt. 11._____

12. When individual countries specialize, (a) nominal GDP decreases (b) deflation results (c) world output increases (d) all of the previous 12._____

13. Which of the following can be used to restrict free trade? (a) quotas (b) tariffs (c) domestic content requirements (d) all of the previous 13._____

14. Statistical discrepancy (a) measures the error in the balance-of-payments data (b) measures the trade deficit (c) measures real GDP (d) measures how much money is lost in imports through quotas. 14._____

15. Which of the following countries exports the least value of goods? (a) the United States (b) Canada (c) Mexico (d) Panama 15._____

16. The exchange rate is determined by (a) the World Trade Organization (b) the interaction of demand and supply for currencies (c) Congress (d) none of the previous. 16._____

17. Which of the following countries receives the most goods from the United States? (a) Canada (b) Honduras (c) Japan (d) Mexico. 17._____

18. Once the value of the dollar was no longer tied to gold (a) inflation exploded (b) the dollar remained constant (c) the dollar began to float (d) the country went through the Great Depression

18. _____

19. Which of the following would the financial account track? (a) A Massachusetts-based company buys stock in a company based in Wyoming. (b) A mother in Idaho buys stock in IBM for her daughter. (c) A grandmother gives her grandson a U.S. government bond for his birthday. (d) A British company engages in a hostile takeover of a Texas company.

19. _____

20. Trade restrictions can cause (a) livelier economic progress (b) decreased competition (c) low transaction costs (d) an increase in U.S. GDP.

20. _____

Part 3—Short Answer

Directions: Read the following questions, and write your response.

21. What is the largest category of goods that is imported by the United States? What do you own that might fall into this category?

22. Discuss at least two disadvantages of trade restrictions.

Part 4—Critical Thinking

Directions: Imagining that you are the president of a small European country, answer the following questions.

23. How would you determine what to produce?

24. Would you want your country to specialize in producing certain goods? Why or why not?

25. Why would it benefit your country to trade with other nations? Why or why not?

Lesson 19.1 Developing Economies & Industrial Market Economies

Part 1—True or False

Directions: Place a *T* for True or an *F* for False in the Answers column to show whether each of the following statements is true or false.

Answers

1. Child labor is common in developing countries.   1._____

2. Less than a third of GDP in developing countries stems from agriculture.   2._____

3. Most of the labor force in developing countries works in industrial production.   3._____

4. Most people in developing countries have steady, full-time jobs.   4._____

5. American farmers grow enough to feed the nation but not enough to export.   5._____

6. Attitudes about family size are changing in many developing countries.   6._____

7. Some workers in developing countries simply do not have the education to know how to   7._____
   produce more.

8. Although many people in developing countries are unemployed, not many are underemployed. 8._____

9. More people live in industrial market countries than in developing countries.   9._____

Part 2—Multiple Choice

Directions: In the Answers column, write the letter that represents the word, or group of words, that correctly completes the statement or answers the question.

Answers

10. What is the most common measure of living standards? (a) the unemployment rate (b) income   10._____
    per family (c) GDP per capita (d) the number of college-educated people

11. Why are fertility rates higher in developing countries? (a) Children are viewed as social   11._____
    insurance for their parents. (b) Children are viewed as a source of farm labor. (c) Parents
    compensate for high infant mortality rates. (d) all of the previous

12. What is the primary cause of death for children in developing countries? (a) polio (b) cholera 12._____
    (c) malnutrition (d) AIDS/HIV

13. Which of the following characterizes the cycle of low income that is so common in developing 13._____
    countries? (a) Workers save less because they earn less. (b) Businesses can invest in more
    human capital because so many people need jobs. (c) Adults are even better suited for
    employment because their parents paid for an education. (d) none of the previous

14. Which of the following contributes to the lower productivity rates in developing countries? 14._____
    (a) efficient use of labor (b) less education (c) too many entrepreneurs (d) all of the previous

15. Which of the following is usually true of a developing country? (a) high unemployment rates 15._____
    (b) slow population growth (c) lower rates of illiteracy (d) hardly any underemployment

16. Which of the following countries has the highest life expectancy? (a) Africa (b) Sierra Leone 16._____
    (c) Haiti (d) Japan

17. Why is labor productivity low in developing countries? (a) There is less interest in getting a 17._____
    good job. (b) There is less physical and human capital. (c) International competition hinders
    developing countries' labor productivity. (d) all of the previous

18. Which of the following is true about industrial market countries? (a) low GDP per capita   18._____
    (b) high rates of illiteracy (c) slow population growth (d) high unemployment rates

19. Which of the following is not an industrial market country? (a) the United States (b) Australia   19._____
    (c) India (d) Japan

Part 3—Short Answer

Directions: Read the following questions, and write your response.

20. What is the most common measure of living standards worldwide?

21. What portion of the world's population resides in China and India?

22. What portion of the world's 6.5 billion population live in industrialized market countries?

23. What accounts for the high birth rates of developing countries?

24. Why is underemployment prevalent in developing countries?

Part 4—Critical Thinking

Directions: Read the following questions, and write your response

25. What characteristics are true of the world's poorest people?

26. What is the vicious cycle of poverty, and how can it be broken?

27. Other than customer service and telemarketing work, suggest other types of employment that could
    potentially be exported from industrialized market countries to developing countries.

Lesson   19.2   Foreign Trade, Foreign Aid, & Economic Development

Part 1—True or False

Directions: Place a *T* for True or an *F* for False in the Answers column to show whether each of the following statements is true or false.

Answers

1. A major source of foreign exchange in some developing countries is the money sent home by migrants who find jobs in industrial countries.   1._____

2. Foreign aid always takes the form of money.   2._____

3. Job opportunities are better in industrial economies as opposed to developing countries.   3._____

4. Development aid is aid from an organization that gets funds from a group of countries.   4._____

5. Economic development usually involves a shift from agricultural products to manufacturing more complex products.   5._____

6. By nature, bilateral funding cannot be tied to purchases of goods and services from the donor nation.   6._____

7. Some foreign aid does not need to be repaid.   7._____

8. Many poor countries rely on foreign aid for their financial capital.   8._____

9. Economists favor import substitution over export promotion.   9._____

10. Foreign aid adds to national saving as opposed to simply substituting for national saving.   10._____

Part 2—Multiple Choice

Directions: In the Answers column, write the letter that represents the word, or group of words, that correctly completes the statement or answers the question.

Answers

11. What is the brain drain? (a) People in developing countries cannot afford to get a college education. (b) Educated people from a developing country move to industrial market countries. (c) Those in developing countries are threatened by educated immigrants. (d) none of the previous   11._____

12. Which of the following is a goal of the U.S. Agency for International Development (USAID)? (a) to provide loans and not technical assistance (b) to decrease America's involvement in other nations' affairs (c) to focus on increasing manufacturing in developing countries (d) to improve living standards in the developing world   12._____

13. What is the most recent trend concerning foreign aid? (a) It is given to foreign governments to disperse. (b) The amount of foreign aid is decreasing drastically. (c) More than half goes to countries through private channels. (d) It must be approved by the citizens of a foreign country.   13._____

14. Why did import substitution become so popular? (a) It was popular with those who supplied labor, capital, and other resources to the protected domestic industries. (b) Companies created a demand for products that were not already present. (c) Countries wanted to phase out the use of foreign exchange. (d) all of the previous   14._____

15. Other than the poor for whom it is intended, who does foreign aid benefit much of the time? (a) foreign government officials (b) USAID administrators (c) foreign factory workers (d) foreign company owners   15._____

16. Suppose that the United States grants foreign aid to a country in Africa. Which of the following best describes this? (a) multilateral aid (b) bilateral aid (c) country-to-country aid (d) brain drain

16. _____

17. What was a drawback of import substitution? (a) domestic industries were not protected (b) companies had no choice but to sell products at lower prices (c) consumers were faced with lower quality products (d) all of the previous

17. _____

18. How may a country be affected by receiving foreign aid? (a) increases people's ability to support themselves (b) standard of living increases (c) its immediate need for imported food will decline (d) all of the previous

18. _____

19. Which of the following countries have pursued import substitution policies? (a) Canada (b) the United States (c) Great Britain (d) Argentina

19. _____

20. Which of the following is true of export promotion? (a) focuses on producing goods for domestic sale (b) makes producers become more efficient (c) focuses on the production of complex products first and foremost (d) requires more government intervention than does import substitution

20. _____

Part 3—Short Answer

Directions: Read the following questions, and write your response.

21. How do developing countries generate the foreign exchange necessary to import necessary capital and technology?

23. What is the brain drain, and how does this hurt developing economies?

24. What is the mission of USAID?

Part 4—Critical Thinking

Directions: Read the following questions, and write your response.

25. What are some pros and cons of the strategy of import substitution?

26. How is export promotion a strategy that supports free markets?

Lesson ⬤19.3 Rules of the Game, Transition Economies, & Convergence

Part 1—True or False

Directions: Place a *T* for True or an *F* for False in the Answers column to show whether each of the following statements is true or false.

Answers

1. Rules of the game are vital for economic development. 1._____

2. A stable political climate promotes investment in the economy. 2._____

3. Consumer goods in centrally planned economies are often priced below the market-clearing level, which creates shortages. 3._____

4. Russian privatization was a fairly smooth process. 4._____

5. Most prices in centrally planned economies are established by market forces. 5._____

6. In order for privatization to work well, the general population must perceive it to be fair. 6._____

7. There is no evidence that the convergence theory is true. 7._____

8. Central plans are replacing markets in a growing number of countries around the world. 8._____

9. Prices in centrally planned economies usually are inflexible. 9._____

10. With central planning, any "profit" earned by a state enterprise is appropriated by the state. 10._____

Part 2—Multiple Choice

Directions: In the Answers column, write the letter that represents the word, or group of words, that correctly completes the statement or answers the questions.

Answers

11. What does the convergence theory argue? (a) Developing countries will never reach the level of more advanced countries. (b) Developing countries will eventually bypass more advanced countries in terms of technological breakthroughs. (c) Developing countries can grow faster than more advanced countries. (d) Developing countries must make their own technological advances. 11._____

12. Which of the following best defines soft budget constraints? (a) in free market economies, the loans that must be taken out to cover lost money (b) the process of turning public enterprises into private ones (c) in centrally planned economies, the budget condition faced by state enterprises that are subsidized when they lose money (d) none of the previous 12._____

13. Which of the following is **not** an example of a rule of the game? (c) a country's population (b) a country's laws (c) a country's beliefs (d) a country's customs 13._____

14. Which of the following trends have been noted most recently in developing countries? (a) The child labor force is growing. (b) Work conditions are improving. (c) Trade barriers are becoming stricter. (d) World income is steadily decreasing. 14._____

15. Which is a feature of developing countries? (a) peaceful conditions (b) physical infrastructure deficiencies (c) strong, formal rules of the game (d) none of the previous 15._____

16. What is the opposite of privatization? (a) entrepreneurship (b) soft budget constraints (c) nationalization (d) democracy 16._____

17. Which of the following is **not** an example of physical infrastructure? (a) power electricity plants (b) automobiles (c) highways (d) sanitation facilities   17._____

18. Why is it difficult for developing countries to achieve convergence? (a) There is not enough human capital. (b) They experience brain drain. (c) Birth rates in those countries are very high. (d) all of the previous   18._____

19. Most centrally planned economies that are trying to privatize face what problem? (a) Their laws guiding rules of conduct for market participants are too strict. (b) They have no history of market interaction. (d) They are not supported by other countries, so they usually fail. (d) all of the previous   19._____

20. What effect might a civil war have on a country? (a) an increase in investment (b) a decreased standard of living (c) an increase in productivity (d) all of the previous   20._____

Part 3—Short Answer

Directions: Read the following questions, and write your response.

21. What comprises a country's physical infrastructure?

22. Why is covering costs and turning a profit not necessarily the goal of centrally planned economies?

23. What makes privatization a difficult process in many instances?

Part 4—Critical Thinking

Directions: Read the following questions, and write your response.

24. Should a world organization impose standard "rules of the game" for all countries? Why or why not?

25. Will economies of the world eventually converge? Why or why not?

26. What accounts for the differences in human capital across countries?

Chapter ⬤19 Review

Part 1—True or False

Directions: Place a *T* for True or an *F* for False in the Answers column to show whether each of the following statements is true or false.

Answers

1. Today, most foreign aid is given to foreign governments to disperse.   1._____

2. AIDS/HIV is the primary cause of death for children in developing countries.   2._____

3. Export promotion causes producers to become more efficient.   3._____

4. The convergence theory argues that developing countries can grow faster than more advanced   4._____
   countries.

5. Labor productivity is low in developing countries because there is less physical and human   5._____
   capital.

6. Child labor is illegal in every country.   6._____

7. Foreign aid may take many forms, including money.   7._____

8. Industrial market economies enjoy a high GDP per capita.   8._____

9. With central planning, any "profit" earned by a state enterprise is put into welfare programs.   9._____

10. Foreign aid does not always benefit a country's population first and foremost.   10._____

Part 2—Multiple Choice

Directions: In the Answers column, write the letter that represents the word, or group of words, that correctly completes the statement or answers the question.

Answers

11. The U.S. Agency for International Development (USAID) (a) distributes foreign aid to   11._____
    governments (b) pushes to decrease U.S. involvement in foreign nations (c) tries to convert
    central planning economies into industrial market economies (d) improves living standards in
    the developing world

12. Which of the following is an example of a "rule of the game"? (a) type of government   12._____
    (b) customs (c) level of education (d) population

13. Soft budget constraints are (a) the effects that occur when centrally planned economies try to   13._____
    become industrial market economies (b) the budget condition faced by state enterprises that
    are subsidized when they lose money in centrally planned economies (c) the results of the
    U.S. budget deficit (d) none of the previous

14. Which of the following is an example of physical infrastructure? (a) food stuffs (b) cars   14._____
    (c) highways (d) all of the previous

15. Which of the following is an industrial market country? (a) Australia (b) South Africa (c) the   15._____
    Philippines (d) India

16. What is the most common measure of living standard? (a) GDP per capita (b) inflation   16._____
    (c) productivity per worker (d) the number of people who receive welfare benefits

17. Brain drain occurs when (a) educated people from a developing country move to industrial market countries (b) educated people from an industrial market country move to developing countries (c) more than 50 percent of a country's population does not have a high school degree (d) governments prevent adults from attaining higher education   17.____

18. Which of the following countries have pursed import substitution policies? (a) the United States (b) Argentina (c) Ireland (c) Japan   18.____

19. Which of the following countries has the highest life expectancy? (a) Uganda (b) Iraq (c) the United States (d) Japan   19.____

20. If the United States grants foreign aid to Honduras, it has engaged in an act of (a) multilateral aid (b) convergence (c) bilateral aid (d) unilateral aid   20.____

Part 3—Short Answer

Directions: Read the following questions, and write your response.

21. Compare industrial market countries to developing countries.

22. What is import substitution, and who has engaged in it? Why did it become popular?

Part 4—Critical Thinking

23. What might improve the negative effects of foreign aid on developing countries?

24. If the WTO made all trade restrictions illegal worldwide, who would this hurt? Who would this help?

25. Should the U.S. standard wage have any influence on the wages paid to workers in developing countries that make U.S. products?